Stories of Famous Regiments by Philip Warner

Index Of Contents

I0139614

Introduction

This book includes but a small number of the many hundreds of feats of outstanding bravery performed by British soldiers. Some are well known, some scarcely known at all, and yet others have never been recorded, apart from a bare mention in a regimental diary. Equally, some of the regiments are world famous; others have disappeared in a welter of amalgamations, although it is still possible (usually) to trace one battalion - or even company - which is a direct descendant of a much larger and more renowned predecessor. One fact will sing out like a trumpet to those who read this book and that is whatever the century, whatever the country, and whatever the task, the British soldier is second to none. There are brave men in all countries and not only brave men but enduring, flexible, ingenious, and resilient men too; however, in the annals of history the British soldier has a record which is unsurpassed. It will not escape the reader's notice that for a regiment to perform a brave deed it needs first-class, or at least plentiful, opposition. A regiment can only prove itself in daunting circumstances; every tribute to a British regiment in this book in greater or lesser degree reflects some credit on its opponents.

Regiment is a broad term. It is best understood by taking a quick look at its origins. With the development of gunpowder in the sixteenth century the army was loosely organized into a number of companies of varying strength, some with as few as a hundred and fifty men; others with double that number. Each company had a colour or ensign and in later military history we often find accounts of stirring action to save a colour or to capture one from the enemy. There was, of course, nothing new in the sacred nature of the colour. Throughout history it has been the hope and rallying point of the unit and men have not hesitated to sacrifice their lives to preserve it.

Experience showed that if several companies were grouped together this formed a convenient battle unit. Such groupings were called 'regiments', and numbered up to three thousand men; companies, however, still carried their own colours.

In the sixteenth century, when Gustavus Adolphus of Sweden was organizing his army with great skill, it was noted that his regiments did not exceed a thousand in number. His organization was soon copied by other nations, including our own. The new units, which usually consisted of ten companies of one hundred men each, were commanded by a colonel. His second-in-command was called the sergeant-major but later this became major. 'Sergeant-major' reappeared later as a non-commissioned rank. As more men were needed for various wars, second regiments were raised. These became known as the 2nd —. In the present century, principally in the First World War, regiments were rapidly expanded; in the infantry the extra regiments were known as 'battalions' and one regiment acquired forty-two. Specialist arms were usually called 'corps' although some of these, such as the King's Royal Rifle Corps, were really regiments. At the other end of the scale was the Royal Regiment of Artillery, which ultimately became enormous and consisted of regiments within a regiment, for instance, 15 Field Regiment. For most of the actions in this book it may be assumed that the deeds described were performed by a part of a regiment, whether or not it was designated as such at the time. Sometimes a number of small detachments from different units would make up a balanced force. The Light Brigade which charged in the Crimean War was less than three-quarters of the strength of a normal regiment; the term 'brigade' now means a group of three regiments. Obviously numbers vary from time to time to meet operational requirements - or even changes in recruiting - and present-day numbers are no guide to the formations of the past.

Unfortunately efficiency has not been the main reason for the reshaping of the regimental system. The combination of apparent economy and tidier planning has swept away many a regimental name which once stirred the blood. This is no place to comment on present-day organization other than to say that the lesson of military history has been that a man tended to perform better in an easily recognizable and memorable unit than in a large organization composed of several extinguished regiments with no clear territorial association or historically renowned number. It would be invidious to mention names but readers of the following pages may sometimes look for a famous regiment among modern army lists - and look in vain. To quote but one - where is the Rifle Brigade? It does in fact exist: it is the third battalion of the Royal Green Jackets but for a time it did not exist at all. And now to the actions that made some of the living and dead regiments famous.

Chapter I

The Napoleonic Wars

QUATRE BRAS

The length and impact of the Napoleonic wars is, not surprisingly, little known nowadays. But one hundred and fifty years ago it was appreciated well enough by people who were still suffering from the after effects. The war with France had begun in 1793 and it continued with short breaks until 1815. During that period there were several terrifying disasters and it often seemed that England might lose the war. The worst stage of the war was from 1803 to 1815. For the first two and a quarter years of that period Napoleon had 120,000 men on the French coast with a flotilla of boats, waiting to invade this country.

In a war of such size there were inevitably many heroic actions. One of these concerns the Rifle Brigade. In 1801 a group of riflemen was formed to experiment with the new Baker rifle. The rifle was modelled on the Hessian weapon and produced by a Whitechapel gunsmith. It had a range of three hundred yards, fired one round a minute, and had a twenty-three-inch-long bayonet. The regiment, then known as the 95th, wore a green uniform like that of gamekeepers. The colonel of the regiment, Colonel Coote Manningham, trained his men to be self-reliant, enduring and able to move and fight in small groups.

In the second battalion was a young officer, Captain Sir John Kincaid. In 1811 he was in the Peninsula campaign. On 12 March Massena was retreating and Wellington was following him up closely. Kincaid wrote of his experiences at this time in the first extract given here.

Later Kincaid's regiment was in Belgium. Napoleon had escaped from Elba and rejoined a now revitalized French army.

On 15 June 1813 he advanced on allied armies in Belgium. Blucher had 80,000 men but Wellington had only 7,000 (to confront 19,000 French). Napoleon beat Blucher at Ligny, then turned on Wellington at Quatre Bras. Before the end of the fighting Wellington had acquired substantial reinforcements but his victory was due to skill and not to numbers...

I was one of a crowd of skirmishers who were enabling the French ones to carry the news of their own defeat through a thick wood, at an infantry canter, when I found myself all at once within a few yards of one of their regiments in line, which opened such a fire, that had I not, rifleman like, taken instant advantage of the cover of a good fir tree, my name would have unquestionably been transmitted to posterity by that night's gazette. And, however opposed it may be to the usual system of drill, I will maintain, from that day's experience, that the cleverest method of teaching a recruit to stand at attention, is to place him behind a tree and fire balls at him; as, had our late worthy disciplinarian, Sir David Dundas, himself, been looking on, I think that even he must have admitted that he never saw any one stand so fiercely upright as I did behind mine, while the balls were rapping into it as fast as if a fellow had been hammering a nail on the opposite side, not to mention the numbers that were whistling past, within an eighth of an inch of every part of my body, both before and behind, particularly in the vicinity of my nose, for which the upper part of the tree could barely afford protection.

This was a last and desperate stand made by their rearguard, for their own safety, immediately above the town, as their sole chance of escape depended upon their being able to hold the post until the only bridge across the river was clear of the other fugitives. But they could not hold it long enough: for, while we were undergoing a temporary sort of purgatory in their front, our comrades went working round their flanks, which quickly sent them flying, with us intermixed, at full cry, down the streets.

Whether in love or war, I have always considered that the pursuer has a decided advantage over the pursued. In the first, he may gain and cannot lose; but in the latter, when one sees his enemy at full speed before him, one has such a peculiar conscious sort of feeling that he is on the right side, that I would not exchange places for any consideration.

When we reached the bridge, the scene became exceedingly interesting, for it was choked up by the fugitives who were, as usual, impeding each other's progress, and we did not find that the application of our swords to those nearest to us tended at all towards lessening their disorder, for it induced about a hundred of them to rush into an adjoining house for shelter, but that was getting regularly out of the frying-pan into the fire, for the house happened to be really in flames, and too hot to hold them, so that the same hundred were quickly seen unkennelling again, half-cooked, into the very jaws of their consumers.

John Bull, however, is not a bloodthirsty person, so that those who could not better themselves, had only to submit to a simple transfer of personal property to ensure his protection. We, consequently, made many prisoners at the bridge, and followed their army about a league beyond it, keeping up a flying fight until dark.

Just as Mr Simmons and myself had crossed the river, and were talking over the events of the day, not a yard asunder, there was a Portuguese soldier in the act of passing between us, when a cannon-ball plunged into his belly — his head doubled down to his feet and he stood for a moment in that posture before he rolled over a lifeless lump.

March 13th - Arrived on the hill above Condacia in time to see that handsome little town in flames. Every species of barbarity continued to mark the enemy's retreating steps. They burnt every town or village through which they passed, and if we entered a church, which, by accident, had been spared, it was to see the murdered bodies of the peasantry on the altar.

While Lord Wellington, with his staff, was on a hill a little in front of us, waiting the result of a flank-movement which he had directed, some of the enemy's sharpshooters stole, unperceived, very near to him and began firing, but, fortunately, without effect. We immediately detached a few of ours to meet them, but the others ran off on their approach.

We lay by our arms until towards evening, when the enemy withdrew a short distance behind Condacia, and we closed up to them. There was a continued popping between the advanced posts all night.

March 14th - Finding, at daylight, that the enemy still continued to hold the strong ground before us, some divisions of the army were sent to turn their flanks, whilst ours attacked them in front. We drove them from one stronghold to another, over a large track of very difficult country, mountainous and rocky, and thickly intersected with stone walls, and were involved in one continued hard skirmish from daylight until dark. This was the most harassing day's fighting that I had ever experienced.

Daylight left the two armies looking at each other, near the village of Illama. The smoking roofs of the houses showed that the French had just quitted and, as usual, set fire to it, when the company to which I belonged was ordered on piquet there for the night. After posting our sentries, my brother-officer and myself had the curiosity to look into a house, and were shocked to find in it a mother and her child dead, and the father, with three more, living, but so much reduced by famine as to be unable to remove themselves from the flames. We carried them into the open air, and offered the old man our few remaining crumbs of biscuit, but he told us that he was too far gone to benefit by them, and begged that we would give them to his children. We lost no time in examining such of the other houses as were yet safe to enter, and rescued many more individuals from one horrible death, probably to reserve them for another equally so, and more lingering, as we had nothing to give them, and marched at daylight the following morning.

Our post that night was one of terrific grandeur. The hills behind were in a blaze of light with the British camp-fires, as were those in our front with the French ones. Both hills were abrupt and lofty, not above eight hundred yards asunder, and we were in the burning village in the valley between. The roofs of houses every instant falling in, and the sparks and flames ascending to the clouds. The streets were strewed with the dying and the dead, - some had been murdered and some killed in action, which, together with the half-famished wretches whom we had saved from burning, contributed in making it a scene which was well calculated to shake a stout heart, as was proved in the instance of one of our sentries, a well-known 'devil-may-care' sort of fellow. I know not what appearances the burning rafters might have reflected on the neighbouring trees at the time, but he had not been long on his post before he came running into the piquet, and swore, by all the saints in the calendar, that he saw six dead Frenchmen advancing upon him with hatchets over their shoulders!

We found by the buttons on the coats of some of the fallen foe, that we had this day been opposed to the French ninety-fifth regiment (the same number as we were then) and cut off several of them, which I preserved as trophies.

March 15th - We overtook the enemy a little before dark this afternoon. They were drawn up behind the Ceira, at Foz D'Aronce, with their rearguard, under Marshal Ney, imprudently posted on our side of the river, a circumstance which Lord Wellington took immediate advantage of; and, by a furious attack, dislodged them, in such confusion, that they blew up the bridge before half of their own people had time to get over. Those who were thereby left behind, not choosing to put themselves to the pain of being shot, took to the river, which received them so hospitably that few of them ever quitted it. Their loss, on this occasion, must have been very great, and, we understood, at the time, that Ney had been sent to France, in disgrace, in consequence of it.

About the middle of the action, I observed some inexperienced light troops rushing up a deep road-way to certain destruction, and ran to warn them out of it, but I only arrived in time to partake the reward of their indiscretion, for I was instantly struck with a musket ball above the left ear, which deposited me, at full length, in the mud.

I know not how long I lay insensible, but, on recovering, my first feeling was for my head, to ascertain if any part of it was still standing, for it appeared to me as if nothing remained above the mouth; but, after repeated applications of all my fingers and thumbs to the doubtful parts, I, at length, proved to myself, satisfactorily, that it had rather increased than diminished by the concussion; and, jumping on my legs, and hearing, by the whistling of the balls from both sides, that the rascals who had got me into the scrape had been driven back and left me there, I snatched my cap, which had saved my life, and which had been spun off my head to the distance of ten or twelve yards, and joined them, a short distance in the rear, when one of them, a soldier of the sixtieth, came and told me that an officer of ours had been killed, a short time before, pointing to the spot where I myself had fallen, and that he had tried to take his jacket off, but that the advance of the enemy had prevented him. I told him that I was the one that had been killed, and that I was deucedly obliged to him for his kind intentions, while I felt still more so to the enemy for their timely advance, otherwise, I have no doubt but my friend would have taken a fancy to my trousers also, for I found that he had absolutely unbuttoned my jacket.

There is nothing so gratifying to frail mortality as a good dinner when most wanted and least expected. It was perfectly dark before the action finished, but, on going to take advantage of the fires which the enemy had evacuated, we found their soup- kettles in full operation, and every man's mess of biscuit lying beside them, in stockings, as was the French mode of carrying them; and it is needless to say how unceremoniously we proceeded to do the honours of the feast. It ever after became a saying among the soldiers, whenever they were on short allowance, 'Well, damn my eyes, we must either fall in with the French or the commissary to-day, I don't care which.'

Quatre Bras, at that time, consisted of only three or four houses; and, as its name betokens, I believe, stood at the junction of four roads; on one of which we were moving; a second, inclined to the right; a third, in the same degree, to the left; and the fourth, I conclude, must have gone backwards; but, as I had not an eye in that direction, I did not see it.

The village was occupied by some Belgians, under the Prince of Orange, who had an advanced post in a large farmhouse, at the foot of the road, which inclined to the right; and a part of his division, also, occupied the wood on the same side.

Lord Wellington, I believe, after leaving us at Waterloo, galloped on to the Prussian position at Ligny, where he had an interview with Blucher, in which they concerted measures for their mutual co-operation. When we arrived at Quatre Bras, however, we found him in a field near the Belgian out-post; and the enemy's guns were just beginning to play upon the spot where he stood, surrounded by a numerous staff.

We halted for a moment on the brow of the hill; and as Sir Andrew Barnard galloped forward to the headquarters group, I followed, to be in readiness to convey any orders to the battalion. The moment we approached, Lord Fitzroy Somerset, separating himself from the duke, said, ' Barnard, you are wanted instantly; take your battalion and endeavour to get possession of that village,' pointing to one on the face of the rising ground, down which the enemy were moving; ' but if you cannot do that, secure that wood on the left, and keep the road open for communication with the Prussians.' We instantly moved in the given direction; but, ere we had got half-way to the village, we had the mortification to see the enemy throw such a force into it, as rendered any attempt to retake it, with our numbers, utterly hopeless; and as another strong body of them were hastening towards the wood, which was the second object pointed out to us, we immediately brought them to action, and secured it. In moving to that point, one of our men went raving mad, from excessive heat. The poor fellow cut a few extraordinary capers, and died in the course of a few minutes.

While our battalion-reserve occupied the front of the wood, our skirmishers lined the side of the road, which was the Prussian line of communication. The road itself, however, was crossed by such a shower of balls, that none but a desperate traveller would have undertaken a journey on it. We were presently reinforced by a small battalion of foreign light troops, with whose assistance we were in hopes to have driven the enemy a little further from it; but they were a raw body of men, who had never before been under fire; and, as they could not be prevailed upon to join our skirmishers, we could make no use of them whatever. Their conduct, in fact, was an exact representation of Mathews's ludicrous one of the American militia, for Sir Andrew Barnard repeatedly pointed out to them which was the French and which our side; and, after explaining that they were not to fire a shot until they joined our skirmishers, the word 'March!' was given; but march, to them, was always the signal to fire, for they stood fast, and began blazing away, chiefly at our skirmishers too; the officers commanding whom were every time sending back to say that we were shooting them; until we were, at last, obliged to be satisfied with whatever advantages their appearance could give, as even that was of some consequence, where troops were so scarce.

Buonaparte's attack on the Prussians had already commenced, and the fire of artillery and musketry, in that direction, was tremendous; but the intervening higher ground prevented us from seeing any part of it.

The plain to our right, which we had just quitted, had, likewise, become the scene of a sanguinary and unequal contest. Our division, after we left it, developed into line, and, in advancing, met and routed the French infantry; but, in following up their advantage, they encountered a furious charge of cavalry, and were obliged to throw themselves into squares to receive it. With the exception of one regiment, however, which had two companies cut to pieces, they were not only successful in resisting the attack, but made awful havoc in the enemy's ranks, who, nevertheless, continued their forward career, and went sweeping past them, like a whirlwind, up to the village of Quatre Bras, to the confusion and consternation of the numerous useless appendages of our army, who were there assembled, waiting the result of the battle.

The forward movement of the enemy's cavalry gave their infantry time to rally; and, strongly reinforced with fresh troops, they again advanced to the attack. This was a crisis in which, according to Buonaparte's theory, the victory was theirs, by all the rules of war, for they held superior numbers, both before and behind us; but the gallant old Picton, who had been trained in a different school, did not choose to confine himself to rules in those matters; despising the force in his rear, he advanced, charged, and routed those in his front, which created such a panic among the others, that they galloped back through the intervals in his division with no other object in view but their own safety. After this desperate conflict, the firing, on both sides, lulled almost to a calm for nearly an hour, while each was busy in renewing their order of battle. The Duke of Brunswick had been killed early in the action, endeavouring to rally his young troops, who were unable to withstand the impetuosity of the French; and, as we had no other cavalry force in the field, the few British infantry regiments present, having to bear the full brunt of the enemy's superior force of both arms, were now considerably reduced in numbers.

The battle, on the side of the Prussians, still continued to rage in an unceasing roar of artillery. About four in the afternoon, a troop of their dragoons came, as a patrol, to inquire how it fared with us, and told us, in passing, that they still maintained their position. Their day, however, was still to be decided, and, indeed, for that matter, so was our own; for, although the firing, for the moment, had nearly ceased, I had not yet clearly made up my mind which side had been the offensive, which the defensive, or which the winning. I had merely the satisfaction of knowing that we had not lost it; for we had met fairly in the middle of a field (or, rather unfairly, considering that they had two to one), and, after the scramble was over, our division still held the ground they fought on. All doubts on the subject, however, began to be removed about five o'clock. The enemy's artillery once more opened; and, on running to the brow of the hill, to ascertain the cause, we perceived our old light-division general, Count Alten, at the head of a fresh British division, moving gallantly down the road towards us. It was, indeed, a joyful sight; for, as already mentioned, our division had suffered so severely that we could not help looking forward to a renewal of the action, with such a disparity of force, with considerable anxiety; but this reinforcement gave us new life, and, as soon as they came near enough to afford support, we commenced the offensive, and, driving in the skirmishers opposed to us, succeeded in gaining a considerable portion of the position originally occupied by the enemy, when darkness obliged us to desist. In justice to the foreign battalion, which had been all day attached to us, I must say that, in this last movement, they joined us cordially, and behaved exceedingly well. They had a very gallant young fellow at their head; and their conduct, in the earlier part of the day, can, therefore, only be ascribed to its being their first appearance on such a stage. Leaving General Alten in possession of the ground which we had assisted in winning, we returned in search of our division, and reached them about eleven at night, lying asleep in their glory, on the field where they had fought, which contained many a bloody trace of the day's work.

The firing, on the side of the Prussians, had altogether ceased before dark, but recommenced, with redoubled fury, about an hour after; and it was then, as we afterwards learnt, that they lost the battle.

We lay down by our arms, near the farmhouse already mentioned, in front of Quatre Bras; and the deuce is in it if we were not in good trim for sleeping, seeing that we had been either marching or fighting for twenty-six successive hours.

An hour before daybreak, next morning, a rattling fire of musketry along the whole line of piquets made every one spring to his arms; and we remained looking as fierce as possible until daylight, when each side was seen expecting an attack, while the piquets were blazing at one another without any ostensible cause: it gradually ceased, as the day advanced, and appeared to have been occasioned by a patrol of dragoons getting between the piquets by accident; when firing commences in the dark it is not easily stopped.

June 17th - As last night's fighting only ceased with the daylight, the scene, this morning, presented a savage unsettled appearance; the fields were strewed with the bodies of men, horses, torn clothing, and shattered cuirasses; and, though no movements appeared to be going on on either side, yet, as occasional shots continued to be exchanged at different points, it kept every one wide awake. We had the satisfaction of knowing that the whole of our army had assembled on the hill behind in the course of the night.

About nine o'clock, we received the news of Blucher's defeat, and of his retreat to Wavre. Lord Wellington, therefore, immediately began to withdraw his army to the position of Waterloo. Sir Andrew Barnard was ordered to remain as long as possible with our battalion, to mask the retreat of the others; and was told, if we were attacked, that the whole of the British cavalry were in readiness to advance to our relief. I had an idea, however, that a single rifle battalion in the midst of ten thousand dragoons, would come but indifferently off in the event of a general crash, and was by no means sorry when, between eleven and twelve o'clock, every regiment had got clear off, and we followed, before the enemy had put anything in motion against us.

After leaving the village of Quatre Bras, and passing through our cavalry, who were formed on each side of the road, we drew up, at the entrance of Genappe, The rain, at that moment, began to descend in torrents, and our men were allowed to shelter themselves in the nearest houses; but we were obliged to turn out again in the midst of it, in less than five minutes, as we found the French cavalry and ours already exchanging shots, and the latter were falling back to the more favourable ground behind Genappe; we, therefore, retired with them, en masse, through the village, and formed again on the rising ground beyond.

While we remained there, we had an opportunity of seeing the different affairs of cavalry; and it did one's heart good to see how cordially the life-guards went at their work; they had no idea of anything but straightforward fighting, and sent their opponents flying in all directions. The only young thing they showed was in every one who got a roll in the mud (and, owing to the slipperiness of the ground, there were many) going off to the rear, according to their Hyde Park custom, as being no longer fit to appear on parade! I thought, at first, that they had been all wounded, but, on finding how the case stood, I could not help telling them that theirs was now the situation to verify the old proverb, 'The uglier the better soldier!'

The roads, as well as the fields, had now become so heavy, that our progress to the rear was very slow; and it was six in the evening before we drew into the position of Waterloo. Our battalion took post in the second line that night, with its right resting on the Namur road, behind La Haye Sainte, near a small mud-cottage, which Sir Andrew Barnard occupied as a quarter. The enemy arrived in front, in considerable force, about an hour after us, and a cannonade took place in different parts of the line, which ended at dark, and we lay down by our arms. It rained excessively hard the greater part of the night; nevertheless, having succeeded in getting a bundle of hay for my horse, and one of straw for myself, I secured the horse to his bundle, by tying him to one of the men's swords stuck in the ground, and, placing mine under his nose, I laid myself down upon it, and never opened my eyes again until daylight.

From Adventures in the Rifle Brigade and Random Shots of a Rifleman by Capt. Sir John Kincaid (Maclaren and Co., 1838)

ALBUERA

The action at Albuera on 11 May 1811 is renowned as the occasion when the Royal Fusiliers fought with great distinction and gallantry, which, of course, they did. However, the 8,000 British present included not only the two Royal Fusiliers battalions but also the Royal Welch Fusiliers, the Worcesters, the East Surreys, the Northamptons, the Buffs, and the Middlesex, the last of whom were thereafter nicknamed the 'Die-hards'. (The Royal Fusiliers are now merged with other fusilier regiments, such as the Royal Northumberland Fusiliers and Lancashire Fusiliers, and are part of the Royal Regiment of Fusiliers; the Royal Welch Fusiliers remain; the Worcesters are now amalgamated with the Sherwood Foresters and are known as the Worcestershire and Sherwood Forester Regiment; the Northamptons are now part of the Royal Anglian Regiment, and the Middlesex have become part of the Queen's Regiment, which also includes the Buffs, the East Surreys, Sussex and former Queen's.)

Albuera is the fiercest, bloodiest and most amazing fight in the mighty drama of the Peninsular war. On May 11, 1811, the English guns were thundering sullenly over Badajos. Wellington was beyond the Guadiana, pressing Marmont; and Beresford, with much pluck but little skill, was besieging the great frontier fortress. Soult, however, a master of war, was swooping down from Seville to raise the siege. On the 14th he reached Villafranca, only thirty miles distant, and fired salvos from his heaviest guns all through the night to warn the garrison of approaching succour. Beresford could not maintain the siege and fight Soult; and on the night of the 13th he abandoned his trenches, burnt his gabions and fascines,* and marched to meet Soult at Albuera, a low ridge, with a shallow river in front, which barred the road to Badajos. As the morning of May 16, 1811, broke, heavy with clouds, and wild with gusty rainstorms, the two armies grimly gazed at each other in stern pause, ere they joined in the wrestle of actual battle.

* Wickerwork baskets and long faggots used to contain earth on the parapet.

All the advantages, save one, were on the side of the French. Soult was the ablest of the French marshals. If he had not Ney's elan in attack, or Massena's stubborn resource in retreat, yet he had a military genius, since Lannes was dead, second only to that of Napoleon himself. He had under his command 20,000 war- hardened infantry, 40 guns, and 4,000 magnificent cavalry, commanded by Latour Maubourg, one of the most brilliant of French cavalry generals. Beresford, the British commander, had the dogged fighting courage, half Dutch and half English, of his name and blood; but as a commander he was scarcely third-rate. Of his army of 30,000, 15,000 were Spanish, half-drilled, and more than half-starved - they had lived for days on horse-flesh - under Blake, a general who had lost all the good qualities of Irish character, and acquired all the bad ones peculiar to Spanish temper. Of Beresford's remaining troop 8,000 were Portuguese; he had only 7,000 British soldiers.

Beresford ought not to have fought. He had abandoned the siege at Badajos, and no reason for giving battle remained. The condition of Blake's men, no doubt, made retreat difficult. They had reached the point at which they must either halt or lie down and die. The real force driving Beresford to battle, however, was the fighting effervescence in his own blood and the warlike impatience of his English troops. They had taken no part in the late great battles under Wellington; Busaco had been fought and Fuentes de Onoro gained without them; and they were in the mood, both officers and men, of fierce determination to fight somebody! This was intimated somewhat roughly to Beresford, and he had not that iron ascendency over his troops Wellington possessed. As a matter of fact he was himself as stubbornly eager to fight as any private in the ranks.

The superiority of Soult's warlike genius was shown before a shot was fired. Beresford regarded the bridge that crossed the Albuera and the village that clustered at the bridge-head as the key of his position. He occupied the village with Alten's German brigade, covered the bridge with the fire of powerful batteries, and held in reserve above it his best British brigade, the fusiliers, under Cole, the very regiments who, four hours later, on the extreme right of Beresford's position, were actually to win the battle. Soult's sure vision, however, as he surveyed his enemies on the evening of the 15th, saw that Beresford's right was his weak point. It was a rough, broken table-land, curving till it looked into the rear of Beresford's line. It was weakly held by Blake and his Spaniards. Immediately in front was a low wooded hill, behind which, as a screen, an attacking force could be gathered.

In the night Soult placed behind this hill the fifth corps, under Gerard, the whole of his cavalry, under Latour Maubourg, and the strength of his artillery. When the morning broke, Soult had men and 30 guns within ten minutes' march of Beresford's right wing, and nobody suspected it. No gleam of colour, no murmur of packed battalions, no ring of steel, no sound of marching feet warned the deluded English general of the battle-storm about to break on his right wing. A commander with such an unexpected tempest ready to burst on the weakest point of his line was by all the rules of war pre-doomed.

At nine o'clock Soult launched an attack at the bridge, the point where Beresford expected him, but it was only a feint. Beresford, however, with all his faults, had the soldierly brain to which the actual thunder of the cannon gave clearness. He noticed that the French battalions supporting the attack on the bridge did not press on closely. As a matter of fact, as soon as the smoke of artillery from the battle raging at the bridge swept over the field, they swung smartly to the left, and at the double hastened to add themselves to the thunderbolt which Soult was launching at Beresford's right. But Beresford, meanwhile, had guessed Soult's secret, and he sent officer after officer ordering and entreating Blake to change front so as to meet Soult's attack on his flank, and he finally rode thither himself to enforce his commands. Blake, however, was immovable through pride, and his men through sheer physical weakness. They could die, but they could not march or deploy. Blake at last tried to change front, but as he did so the French attack smote him. Pressing up the gentle rise, Gerard's men scourged poor Blake's flank with their fire; the French artillery, coming swiftly on, halted every fifty yards to thunder on the unhappy Spaniards; while Latour Maubourg's lancers and hussars, galloping in a wider sweep, gathered momentum for a wild ride on Blake's actual rear.

Beresford tried to persuade the Spaniards to charge as the French were thus circling round them. Shouts and gesticulations were in vain. He was a man of giant height and strength, and he actually seized a Spanish ensign in his iron grip, and carried him bodily, flag and all, at a run for fifty yards towards the moving French lines, and planted him there. When released, however, the bewildered Spaniard simply took to his heels and ran back to his friends, as a terrified sheep might run back to the flock. In half- an-hour Beresford's battle had grown desperate. Two-thirds of the French, in compact order of battle, were perpendicular to his right; the Spaniards were falling into disorder.

Soult saw the victory in his grasp, and eagerly pushed forward his reserves. Over the whole hill, mingled with furious blasts of rain, rolled the tumult of a disorderly and broken fight. Ten minutes more would have enabled Soult to fling Beresford's right, a shattered and routed mass, on the only possible line of retreat, and with the French superiority in cavalry his army would have been blotted out.

The share of the British in the fight consisted of three great attacks delivered by way of counter-stroke to Soult's overwhelming rush on the hill held by Blake. The first attack was delivered by the second division, under Colborne, led by General Stewart in person. Stewart was a sort of British version of Ney, a man of vehement spirit, with a daring that grew even more flame-like in the eddying tumult and tempest of actual battle. He saw Soult's attack crumpling up Blake's helpless battalions, while the flash of the French artillery every moment grew closer. It was the crisis of the fight, and Stewart brought on Colborne's men at a run. Colborne himself, a fine soldier with cool judgment, wished to halt and form his men in order of battle before plunging into the confused vortex of the fight above; but Stewart, full of breathless ardour, hurried the brigade up the hill in column of companies, reached the Spanish right, and began to form line by succession of battalions as they arrived.

At this moment a wild tempest of rain was sweeping over the British as, at the double, they came up the hill; the eddying fog, thick with the smoke of powder, hid everything twenty yards from the panting soldiers. Suddenly the wall of changing fog to their right sparkled into swiftly moving spots of red; it shone the next instant with the gleam of a thousand steel points; above the thunder of the cannon, the shouts of contending men, rose the awful sound of a tempest of galloping hoofs. The French lancers and hussars caught the English in open order, and in five fierce and bloody minutes almost trampled them out of existence! Two-thirds of the brigade went down. The 31st (East Surreys) Regiment flung itself promptly into square, and stood fast - a tiny island, edged with steel and flame, amid the mad tumult; but the French lancers, drunk with excitement, mad with battle fury, swept over the whole slope of the hill. They captured six guns, and might have done yet more fatal mischief but that they occupied themselves in galloping to and fro across the line of their original charge, spearing the wounded.

One lancer charged Beresford as he sat, solitary and huge, on his horse amid the broken English regiments. But Beresford was at least a magnificent trooper; he put the lance aside with one hand, and caught the Frenchman by the throat, lifted him clean from his saddle, and dashed him senseless on the ground! The ensign who carried the colours of the 3rd Buffs covered them with his body till he was slain by a dozen lance-thrusts; the ensign who carried the other colours of the same regiment tore the flag from its staff and thrust it into his breast, and it was found there, stiff with his blood, after the fight. The Spaniards, meanwhile, were firing incessantly but on general principles merely, and into space or into the ranks of their own allies as might happen; and the 29th (Worcesters), advancing to the help of Colborne's broken men, finding the Spaniards in their path and firing into their lines, broke sternly into volleys on them in turn. Seldom has a battlefield witnessed a tumult so distracted and wild.

The first English counter-stroke had failed, but the second followed swiftly. The furious rain and fog which had proved so fatal to Colborne's men for a moment, was in favour of Beresford. Soult, though eagerly watching the conflict, could not see the ruin into which the British had fallen, and hesitated to launch his reserves into the fight. The 31st still sternly held its own against the French cavalry, and this gave time for Stewart to bring up Houghton's brigade. But this time Stewart, though he brought up his men with as much vehemence as before, brought them up in order of battle. The 29th, the 48th (Northamptons), and the 57th (Middlesex) swept up the hill in line, led by Houghton, hat in hand. He fell, pierced by three bullets; but over his dead body, eager to close, the British line still swept. They reached the crest. A deep and narrow ravine arrested their bayonet charge; but with stubborn valour they held the ground they had gained, scourged with musketry fire at pistol-shot distance, and by artillery at fifty yards' range, while a French column smote them with its musketry on their flank. The men fell fast, but fought as they fell. Stewart was twice wounded; Colonel Dutworth, of the 48th, slain; of the 57th, out of 570 men, 430, with their colonel, Inglis, fell. The men, after the battle, were found lying dead in ranks exactly as they fought. "Die hard! my men, die hard!" said Inglis when the bullet struck him; and the 57th have borne the name of "Die hards" ever since. At Inkerman, indeed, more than fifty years afterwards, the "Die hard!" of Inglis served to harden the valour of the 57th in a fight as stern as Albuera itself.

But ammunition began to fail. Houghton's men would not yield, but it was plain that in a few more minutes there would be none of them left, save the dead and the wounded. And at this dreadful moment Beresford, distracted with the tumult and horror of the fight, wavered! He called up Alten's men from the bridge to cover his retreat, and prepared to yield the fatal hill. At this juncture, however, a mind more masterful and daring than his own launched a third British attack against the victorious French and won the dreadful day.

Colonel Hardinge, afterwards famous in Indian battles, acted as quartermaster-general of the Portuguese army; on his own responsibility he organized the third English attack. Cole had just come up the road from Badajos with two brigades, and Hardinge urged him to lead his men straight up the hill; then riding to Abercrombie's brigade, he ordered him to sweep round the flank of the hill. Beresford, on learning of this movement, accepted it, and sent back Alten's men to retake the bridge which they had abandoned.

Abercrombie's men swept to the left of the hill, and Cole, a gallant and able soldier, using the Portuguese regiments in his brigade as a guard against a flank attack of the French cavalry, led his two fusilier regiments, the 7th (Royal Fusiliers) and 23rd (Royal Welch Fusiliers), straight to the crest. At this moment the French reserves were coming on, the fragments of Houghton's brigade were falling back, the field was heaped with carcases, the lancers were riding furiously about the captured artillery, and with a storm of exultant shouts the French were sweeping on to assured victory. It was the dramatic moment of the fight. Suddenly through the fog, coming rapidly on with stern faces and flashing volleys, appeared the long line of Cole's fusiliers on the right of Houghton's staggering groups, while at the same moment Abercrombie's line broke through the mist on their left. As these grim and threatening lines became visible the French shouts suddenly died down. It was the old contest of the British line - 'the thin red line' - against the favourite French attack in column, and the story can only be told in Napier's resonant prose. The passage which describes the attack of the fusiliers is one of the classic passages of English battle literature, and in its syllables can still almost be heard the tread of marching feet, the shrill clangour of smitten steel, and the thunder of the musketry volleys:

"Such a gallant line," says Napier, "arising from amid the smoke, and rapidly separating itself from the confused and broken multitude, startled the enemy's masses, which were increasing and pressing forward as to assured victory; they wavered, hesitated, and then, vomiting forth a storm of fire, hastily endeavoured to enlarge their front, while the fearful discharge of grape from all their artillery whistled through the British ranks. Myers was killed, Cole and the three colonels - Ellis, Blakeney, and Hawkshawe - fell wounded, and the fusilier battalions, struck by the iron tempest, reeled and staggered like sinking ships. Suddenly and sternly recovering, they closed on their terrible enemies, and then was seen with what a strength and majesty the British soldier fights. In vain did Soult, by voice and gesture, animate his Frenchmen; in vain did the hardiest veterans break from the crowded columns and sacrifice their lives to gain time for the mass to open on such a fair field; in vain did the mass itself bear up, and, fiercely striving, fire indiscriminately on friends and foes, while the horsemen, hovering on the flanks, threatened to charge the advancing line.

"Nothing could stop that astonishing infantry. No sudden burst of undisciplined valour, no nervous enthusiasm weakened the stability of their order; their flashing eyes were bent on the dark columns in front, their measured tread shook the ground, their dreadful volleys swept away the head of every formation, their deafening shouts overpowered the dissonant cries that broke from all parts of the tumultuous crowd as slowly and with a horrid carnage it was driven by the incessant vigour of the attack to the farthest edge of the hill. In vain did the French reserves mix with the struggling multitude to sustain the fight; their efforts only increased the irremediable confusion, and the mighty mass, breaking off like a loosened cliff, went headlong down the ascent. The rain flowed after in streams discoloured with blood, and 1800 unwounded men, the remnant of 6000 unconquerable British soldiers, stood triumphant on the fatal hill."

The battle of Albuera lasted four hours; its slaughter was dreadful. Within the space of a few hundred feet square were strewn some 7,000 bodies, and over this Aceldama the artillery had galloped, the cavalry had charged! The 3rd Buffs went into the fight with 24 officers and 750 rank and file; at the roll-call next morning there were only 5 officers and 35 men. One company of the Royal Fusiliers came out of the fight commanded by a corporal; every officer and sergeant had been killed. Albuera is essentially a soldier's fight. The bayonet of the private, not the brain of the general, won it; and never was the fighting quality of our race more brilliantly shown. Soult summed up the battle in words that deserve to be memorable. "There is no beating those troops," he wrote, "in spite of their generals!" "I always thought them bad soldiers," he added, with a Frenchman's love of paradox; "now I am sure of it. For I turned their right, pierced their centre, they were everywhere broken, the day was mine, and yet they did not know it, and would not run!"

VITORIA

In 1813 when Wellington was advancing into Spain, the French made a desperate stand at Vitoria. Here the Gordon Highlanders, who had fought extremely well throughout the campaign added fresh distinction to their reputations. (The Gordons are the 92nd, the 71st were the Highland Light Infantry, now part of the Royal Highland Fusiliers, and the 50th were the Royal West Kent Regiment, now part of the Queen's.)

Early on the 21st [of June] the troops moved from their camps on the Bayas; the centre of the army passed the ridge of the Morillas in its front, and slowly approached the Zadora. Hill, having seized the village of Puebla, passed the river there. The First Brigade of Morilla's Spaniards led up the ascent, their Second Brigade ascended half-way so as to connect the first with the British below; a stubborn fight was maintained on the heights, and Hill, with the rest of his corps, threaded the long defile of Puebla, and won the village of Subijana de Alava on the other side. Having connected his right with the troops on the mountain, he maintained his position, in spite of the efforts of the enemy to dislodge him.

Meanwhile, Wellington had brought the centre divisions down to the Zadora, where they waited till all were ready to attack, when they crossed, not without fighting. By one o'clock, Hill's assault of Subijana de Alava was developed; the smoke and distant sound of artillery far off to the left showed that Graham's attack had also begun. The Third and Seventh Divisions were rapidly moving down to the bridge of Mendoza; the enemy's artillery opened on them, and his light troops commenced a vigorous fire of musketry, while the British riflemen, who had crossed by another bridge, were between the French cavalry and the river, and were engaging their light troops and gunners so closely that the British artillery, from the other side, were unable to distinguish them in their dark uniforms from their foes. This gallant episode enabled part of the Third Division to pass the bridge, while the rest, and the Seventh Division, forded the river higher up. The French abandoned the ground in front of Villodas and the battle, which had slackened, revived with extreme violence. Hill pressed the enemy on the right, the Fourth Division passed the bridge of Nanclares; the sound of Graham's advance became more distinct, and the banks of the Zadora presented a continuous line of fire. King Joseph, finding both his flanks in danger, had given orders to retire by successive masses, and these orders had shaken their confidence, but the Allies were too close for a regular retrograde movement to be made. The Seventh and a brigade of the Third Divisions were engaged with the French right in front of Margarita and Hermandad, and at the same time Wellington sent the rest of the Third Division.

"Come on, my ragged rascals!" cried Picton, who commanded them, as they doubled across the front of both armies to seize an important hill in the centre. General Cole, with the Fourth Division, advanced, and the heavy cavalry galloped up and formed between Cole's right and Hill's left. The French threw out clouds of skirmishers, and fifty guns played with astonishing activity, being answered by several brigades of British artillery. Both sides were surrounded by smoke and dust, and under its cover the French retired to the second ridge, but still holding Arinez on the main road. Picton's troops plunged into that village under a heavy fire of artillery and musketry, and captured three guns; but fresh French troops arrived, and this important post was disputed with terrible obstinacy, till at last the British emerged victorious from the strife. At the same time a conflict was going on at Margarita, till the French guns were driven away and the village carried. The village of Hermandad was also won, and the whole advanced fighting.

Meanwhile the French left, hard pressed in front and flank, retreated towards Vittoria; but the courage of the French soldiers was not quenched, they took advantage of the broken nature of the ground to renew the contest at every favourable point. Reille maintained his post on the Upper Zadora, while more than eighty guns massed together shook the hills and "streamed with fire and smoke, amidst which the dark figures of the French gunners were seen bounding with frantic energy." This terrible cannonade kept the Allies in check, and the battle became stationary. The French generals commenced drawing off their infantry, covered by their resolute cavalry. Joseph, finding the royal road to Bayonne blocked by carriages, indicated the road of Salvatierra as the line of retreat, and the action resolved itself into a running fight and cannonade. The French reached the last defensible height, a mile in front of Vittoria, about six o'clock; "behind the city thousands of carriages and non-combatants, men, women, and children, were crowding together in all the madness of terror, and, as the British shot went booming overhead, the vast concourse started and swerved with a convulsive movement, while a dull and horrid sound of distress arose, but there was no hope, no stay, for army or multitude."

The foregoing account of the general events of the battle is taken from Napier's History, but I will now relate more particularly the part taken by the First Battalion of the Gordon Highlanders in this great victory, as described by an officer who commanded a company that day, a sergeant who was also present, and several others.

It has been remarked that people seldom get their fill of food and fighting on the same day, and when the dawn ushered in the morning of the 21st of June, there was less appearance of breaking fast than of breaking heads, for the bread was hardly baked when the battalion was ordered to be ready to march at a moment's notice; but fortunately they were ordered to fall out for two hours, when they again stood to their arms, and marched along the road to Puebla. They still knew not whether they were to be engaged in pursuing or fighting the enemy, but now all doubt was removed, for the French held the heights above, and they found that they were within three miles of the main body. A smile of satisfaction played on the soldiers' faces - the veterans encouraged the juniors by telling of former fights, some calculated the numbers of the foe, and all made sure of victory. At a halt, arms and ammunition were closely inspected, and while the captain of the First Company was engaged in this duty, a little incident occurred which shows how the natural fear implanted in most natures may be overcome. A young lad, who had never been in action before, told him he was so unwell that he would be obliged to fall out. The captain asked what was the matter, and received for answer, "A sair wame, sir." The captain walked him up to Colonel Cameron, who, divining his real complaint, took the sick man by the shoulder, and, causing him to face the heights of Puebla, pointed to some French sentries on their summit, and asked if he saw them. He replied in the affirmative. "Well, my man," said the colonel, "those fellows are the best doctors in the world for complaints like yours;" and raising his voice, he continued, "and, by Heaven, if I live you shall consult them this day!" The poor fellow rejoined his companions covered with shame, but during the action was one of the keenest spirits in the fray, and ever after his captain had more difficulty in restraining his courage than he had in rousing it at Vittoria. The officer remarks that young soldiers in going into action for the first time should be mixed with old ones, and taught to subdue bodily fear by moral courage, for had this lad been allowed to retire he would ever after have been an unhappy coward, instead of a gallant and respected soldier.

The battalion, having crossed the Zadora, followed the high road leading to Vittoria, till at a turn they first beheld the dark masses of the enemy in order of battle, and our advanced cavalry two or three hundred paces from those of the French. It was a grand spectacle that presented itself. On the right bank Wellington's troops moving to their stations, on the Highlanders' right the Spaniards climbing the steep heights of Puebla, on which the former could see the French posted, supporting strong bodies of infantry, and some artillery in a clump of trees near the base of the hill. Immediately on their front stood the village of Sabijana de Alava, in which, and on a height to its right, were the centre divisions of the opposing army, which, with numbers of cannon, literally covered the country. As the French battalions successively appeared, the sight, instead of damping the courage of the soldiers, seemed to make them more and more delighted, as "with drums beating and music playing, we advanced as if we were going to a common parade or field-day." At about ten o'clock the sound of musketry on the heights announced to warriors that the conflict had begun — first a few shots, then more continued firing, followed by volleys, accompanied by the British cheer or the French "Vive l'Empereur!" Morillo's Spaniards had acted for some time in conjunction with Hill's Corps, and were considered superior to almost all the other Spanish troops, and nearly equal to the Portuguese; they had, however, little confidence in many of their officers, but Morillo was a brave man and capable general, and when he commanded, as on this occasion, they behaved with great spirit; but the superiority in ground, and latterly in numbers, would have given the French a decided advantage, had not the 71st Highland Light Infantry and the Light Companies of the division, both under Cadogan, arrived to their support; yet the field was doubtful. Morillo was wounded, but did not quit the field; and Colonel Cadogan was turning to cheer his followers, and had just repeated "Well done, well done, brave Highlanders," when he fell from his horse, mortally wounded, into the arms of Captain Seton, commanding the Light Company of the 92nd. He was a brave officer, of high promise, and beloved by his regiment.

An' green be our Cadogan's grave
Upon thy field, Vittoria!

From the poem Battle of Vittoria by W. Glen

The position being most important, Villatte's Division was sent to succour the French, and so well did they fight that the Allies could hardly hold their ground, till Hill sent the 50th and 92nd to their assistance; but when they had almost gained the top they were ordered back. They had descended half-way when they were again stopped, and the battalions separated; the 50th proceeded to its original destination on the summit, while the 92nd moved across the face of the hill to drive back a body of 1000 French infantry, which had advanced to form a link in the chain of communication between the troops at the clump of trees and those who were to capture the heights, about 7000 in number. The soldiers of the 50th and 92nd did not much relish this separation, but there was no help for it, and the former clambered up and proceeded along the ridge till they reached the brink of a ravine which ran across the hill, above and to the left of the column which the 92nd were to attack. Here the Spaniards and 71st lay along the face of the hill, engaged in exchanging fire with the enemy's light troops. The 92nd descended a few hundred yards, and directed their march towards their opponents posted on a ridge. They had to pass through fields of wheat taller than the men, over ditches so thickly lined with briar's and thorns that blood trickled down many of the soldiers' legs before they arrived at the base of the ridge. On crossing the last ditch at the foot of the hill, the battalion loaded, the colonel rode along the fine, cautioning his followers both in Gaelic and English to be firm and steady, and on no account to throw away their fire. He urged them to be silent till the order to charge was given, and then to join in the good old British cheer.

Full of hope and joy, the line advanced slowly and firmly, every moment expecting to see the enemy. Not a whisper was heard, till on arriving a short distance from where the foe was originally posted, instead of the expected volley, they found that their antagonists had retired during their advance to another height at some little distance; and with them the hopes of putting the prowess of Frenchman and Scotsman to the test before an audience of 150,000 men had vanished for the time. Just as they crossed the ridge, General the Hon. W. Stewart, commanding the Second Division, arrived. He ordered the battalion to form column at quarter distance, and two Spanish guns to cannonade the enemy at the clump of trees. This drew the fire of a French battery, and a sergeant, corporal, and one or two privates were hit. The General said to Colonel Cameron, "Poor Cadogan is mortally wounded; the French are pushing strong columns towards our right, they must be opposed." Then waving his hand to his front, "It is on the heights of Puebla the battle must be fought; being now senior officer of the First Brigade, you will instantly proceed thither with your battalion, and assume command on the heights. Yield them to none without a written order from Sir Rowland or myself, and defend your position while you have a man remaining." Then, taking a pencil from his pocket, he wrote the order, the shot and shell flying about his head all the time.

Meanwhile Hill had attacked the French in front of Sabijana de Alava with the rest of his corps. He was met with the greatest determination, and the Highlanders from the hill above witnessed the cool bravery of both sides. The British advancing to the muzzles of their opponents' pieces before giving fire, their repeated assaults were foiled by the devoted bravery of the defenders till, by praiseworthy perseverance and gallantry, they carried their point. Before the village was taken, the 92nd had arrived on the heights, and touched the summit half a mile in rear of the post held by the 50th behind the ravine, of which the western slope was in their possession and that of the 71st, while the enemy were on the opposite bank. The enemy was in superior numbers and our position a strong one, but unfortunately the senior officer on the heights, after Cadogan's fall, ordered the 71st to leave it, to cross the ravine and attack the French on the opposite side; and the gallant Light Bobs at once set out on their perilous undertaking. The enemy had two corps of infantry out of sight of the British, and as the 71st moved round the northern slope, these corps kept moving round the southern slope, till, being nearly in rear of the 71st, hoping to kill or capture the whole battalion, they poured volleys on them, making many officers and men bite the dust; and it required all the good military qualities which that regiment is well known to possess, to extricate them from their dangerous situation. They were not sparing of their powder, but against such odds all they could hope for was to be able to rejoin the 50th, and this they endeavoured to do; but the French were trying to prevent them, and had partially turned the left of the 71st, when their friends the 92nd arrived to take part in the struggle.

On reaching the heights, the Gordons halted a minute to close up and take breath, and then, in open columns of companies right in front, hurried along at the double till within two hundred yards of the 50th, when they formed line on the right centre company without halting. As soon as the four leading companies had filed far enough to the right for the centre one to have a clear front, Colonel Cameron placed himself on its left, and, telling the men to be steady and sure and to remember their country ("Socair chinnteach 'illean cuinhuichibh 'ur duthaich"), called to the piper to play "The Camerons' Gathering", and to the officer who led it, "Now push forward double quick and give it them sweetly!"

"During the advance," says the officer, "a dead silence reigned through the ranks, men's thoughts being employed in the business they were engaged in. Animated by the presence of the chief, and the warlike sounds of their favourite bagpipe, the men advanced with a front as firm as the rocks of their native mountains, to meet the foe flushed with a temporary success over their countrymen."

As they approached the 50th, the officers and men of that regiment joined in cheer after cheer, and the Highlanders arrived at the western brink of the ravine just as the French were ascending it. At once they poured down on them a shower of shot, then re-echoed the cheers of their friends, and rapidly loading, and being joined by the other companies, a second volley was sent into the thickest ranks of the enemy, making them fly precipitately down the brow, the living on their feet, the dead rolling over and over. This rapid movement secured a safe retreat to the 71st, who now slowly retired to a position on the right of the 92nd. But the enemy, determined if possible to gain the heights, made another trial; his beaten troops were moved round the western shoulder of the hill, and a fresh body of infantry carried round the southern, to renew the assault. During the interval, rather a remarkable incident took place, a public auction amidst the roar of musketry and artillery! A man named Walsh, whose character was so bad that not a soldier in the company would associate with him, had annoyed his comrades by the abominable language he used during the ascent, and when they arrived near the 50th had shocked them by his blasphemous profanity, when, as the words were in his mouth, and before anyone had heard the sound of a bullet at that point, he fell, shot through the head. Prepared as they were for sudden but honourable death on the battlefield, his comrades were horrified at the idea of his being killed in the very act of uttering a torrent of blasphemy; but though they disliked the man, they felt for his widow and children, and while the battalion was resting after repulsing the French, the pay-sergeant of his company, a corporal and private, asked permission to bring the man's knapsack from the rear, and dispose of its contents for their behoof. The Colonel, pleased with the idea, sanctioned it; the auction began, the bidding was brisk, and £1 11s. was added to his balance and remitted to the widow. The good feeling exhibited by this little interlude attracted the admiration of some officers of the 50th who witnessed it.

Shortly after, the head of the French column began to descend the opposite eminence; some skirmishers kept up a smart fire on them, the rest remained in line behind the brink, sitting down with arms sloped to the rear, the colonel explaining that they were to remain in that posture till the enemy were within twenty paces, then to stand up and give them pepper. His orders were admirably obeyed; not a whisper was heard while the enemy was crossing the ravine, till they arrived close up, when "the silence was broken on our lads resuming their standing position, and giving their first fire." The scene which followed was an animated one, and, after a rough encounter, in which the 50th, 71st and 92nd took part, the French were driven back with considerable loss. A French colonel commanding part of the attack had dismounted before crossing the ravine; he was a very corpulent man, and when they retreated, his pace downhill was like the waddle of a duck, which could not be expected to carry him out of the clutches of a Highlander. He was taken, puffing, panting, and perspiring, "and our lads were ill-mannered enough to indulge in a hearty laugh at his expense. Seeing he was the butt of the group, he good-humouredly joined in the laugh, saying to a 92nd officer as he surrendered his sword, " Mon Dieu, mon Dieu ! what a fool I was to part with my horse! For want of it I am now your merry man."

Again the fugitives were withdrawn, and a third column of attack was formed in order to recover the position which they should never have lost. Although this column was even stronger than the others, masses of infantry being collected to support them, they did not show the same spirit as in the two former cases, their efforts were comparatively feeble, and they were soon repulsed. This the British attributed to the state of affairs in the centre, which had now begun to take an active part in the business of the day.

The efforts of the First Brigade, and their Allies having been successful on the extreme right, where they now held undisputed possession, and where their presence had a material effect on the issue of the battle, they had leisure to look down on the magnificent panorama presented to their view not far below. They could clearly see every eminence bristling with the artillery on both sides vomiting fire and death; thousands of infantry marching against each other; they watched with excited confidence the lines of red coats cheering as they charged, the French firmly waiting with the cry of "Vive l'Empereur!" till the British steel was close, when they sometimes, but not always, gave way. They could see the curling smoke far away to the left, where Graham's Corps was slowly and with difficulty forcing back the French right, and hear the salvos of their distant guns; with the spyglasses which some carried, they watched the hussars cross the river, and could distinguish the combatants and the flashing swords in the terrible charges of the heavy dragoons against the equally brilliant French horse. Gradually they observed, with pride and pleasure, the enemy giving way. The fields were intersected by ditches and hedges, behind which they extended their line. "Often," says the 92nd officer, "during that awful struggle did I witness the British soldiers walk up to the brink of a fence, behind which their opponents were arrayed, and in the most cool and determined manner cross their pieces with the latter before they gave their fire. On these occasions the combat invariably assumed a sanguinary aspect, for the ditches were generally too deep for our men to cross, and the French kept up a smart fire till artillery and cavalry came to dislodge them."

From The Life of a Regiment by Lt Col Greenhill Gardyne (D. Douglas, 1903)

Chapter 2

Actions in the Crimea

The first extracts here, which describe the little-known but effective charge of the Heavy Brigade and the well-known but useless charge of the Light Brigade, are taken from W, H. Russell's despatches from the Crimea. Russell was The Times correspondent at this period and accompanied the expeditionary force. He infuriated the staff by his frank, critical reports, in which he castigated both the government and the military administration. He was accused of helping the Russians by reporting information useful to them, which he undoubtedly did; however, he assisted the army by influencing public opinion at home and making sure that administrative chaos was remedied.
At the time of these extracts (towards the end of 1854) the allies had won but not properly utilized a victory at the Alma. Subsequently they had besieged Sebastopol on the south side. On 25 October the Russians decided to sweep the allied troops (British, Turkish and French) into the sea. One Russian group was deterred by the steadiness of the Thin Red Line (the Argyll and Sutherland Highlanders), who were in front of Balaclava, another came over Causeway Height and a third were in the valley between the Fedioukine Hills and Causeway Heights. The party crossing the Causeway Heights were countered by General Scarlett's Heavy Brigade. He had eight hundred men to stop three thousand, and did so by the sheer impetus of the charge which he himself led, although sixty-one at the time; he was wounded in five places. 'Heavy' cavalry was made up of Dragoon Guards and Dragoons. They had bigger and stronger horses than light cavalry and were at their best in this sort

of action. His brigade was made up of two squadrons of the 6th Inniskilling Dragoons (now merged into the 9th Inniskilling Dragoon Guards); two squadrons of the 3th (Princess Charlotte of Wales) Dragoon Guards (now the 5th Inniskilling Dragoon Guards); two squadrons of the 2nd (Royal North British) Dragoon Guards (later to be the Scots Greys and now the Royal Scots Dragoon Guards); one squadron of the 4th (Royal Irish) Dragoon Guards (now the 4th/7th Dragoon Guards); and one squadron of the 1st (Royal) Regiment of Dragoons (now the Blues and Royals).

The Light Brigade which was no less brave and resourceful, though scandalously mishandled, consisted of the 4th Light Dragoons (now the Queen's Royal Irish Hussars) ; the 8th Light Dragoons (now also QRIH); the nth Hussars (now forming with the 10th the Royal Hussars); the 13th Light Dragoons (which has become the 13th/18th Hussars); and the 17th Lancers (which is now the 17/21st Lancers). The total number of men was 673 of which 247 became casualties; 113 were killed, many of them on the way back, by Cossack musketeers.

The Crimean War consisted of considerably more than a few cavalry charges and some heroic nursing by Florence Nightingale. It went on for over two years and far greater courage and endurance was shown in the later stages outside Sebastopol than had ever been shown in the more publicized earlier events. This is shown by the account of a small part of the work of the Royal Sappers and Miners (later to be the Royal Engineers).

The final extract in this section is the account by Midshipman E. Wood who would later be awarded the VC. A naval brigade had been formed and not for the first or last time would the royal navy show the landlubbers that it could fight as well as the best regiment. (There are, of course, plenty of soldiers who can show naval personnel a thing or two about handling ships.) Midshipman Wood found army life much to his taste in the Crimea and soon transferred to that service. He rose to become Field Marshal Sir Evelyn Wood, VC. In this extract he describes his experience with the naval scaling party which hoped to assault the Redan - a Russian strongpoint - with ladders.

BALACLAVA

Lord Raglan perceived that the intention of the Russians was to attack Balaklava, and sent orders to Lord Lucan to move down his heavy horse to cover the approaches, and they were just moving from their position near the vineyard and orchard, when his lordship, seeing that a large body of the enemy's cavalry were coming after him over the ridge, rode after them, wheeled them round, and advanced to meet them. We saw Brigadier-General Scarlett ride along in front of his massive squadrons. The Russians - evidently corps d'elite - their light blue jackets embroidered with silver lace, were advancing on their left, at an easy gallop, towards the brow of the hill. A forest of lances glistened in their rear, and several squadrons of grey-coated dragoons moved up quickly to support them as they reached the summit. The instant they came in sight, the trumpets of our cavalry gave out the warning blast which told us all that in another moment we should see the shock of battle beneath our very eyes. Lord Raglan, all his staff and escort, and groups of officers, the Zouaves, French generals and officers, and bodies of French infantry on the height, were spectators of the scene as though they were looking on the stage from the boxes of a theatre. Nearly every one dismounted and sat down, and not a word was said. The Russians advanced down the hill at a slow canter, which they changed to a trot, and at last nearly halted. Their first line was at least double the length of ours - it was three times as deep. Behind them was a similar line, equally strong and compact. They evidently despised their insignificant-looking enemy, but their time was come.

The trumpets rang out again through the valley, and the Greys and Enniskilleners went right at the centre of the Russian cavalry. The space between them was only a few hundred yards; it was scarce enough to let the horses " gather way ", nor had the men quite space sufficient for the full play of their sword arms. The Russian line brought forward each wing as our cavalry advanced, and threatened to annihilate them as they passed on. Turning a little to their left, so as to meet the Russian right, the Greys rushed on with a cheer that thrilled to every heart - the wild shout of the Enniskilleners rose through the air at the same instant. As lightning flashes through a cloud, the Greys and Enniskilleners pierced through the dark masses of Russians. The shock was but for a moment. There was a clash of steel and a light play of sword- blades in the air, and then the Greys and the redcoats disappeared in the midst of the shaken and quivering columns. In another moment we saw them emerging with diminished numbers, and in broken order, charging against the second line. It was a terrible moment. "God help them! they are lost!" was the exclamation of more than one man, and the thought of many. With unabated fire the noble hearts dashed at their enemy. It was a fight of heroes. The first line of Russians, which had been utterly smashed by our charge, and had fled off at one flank and towards the centre, were coming back to swallow up our handful of men. By sheer steel and sheer courage Enniskillener and Scot were winning their desperate way right through the enemy's squadrons, and already grey horses and red coats had appeared right at the rear of the second mass, when, with irresistible force, like one bolt from a bow, the 4th Dragoon Guards, riding straight at the right flank of the Russians, and the 5th Dragoon Guards, following close after the Enniskilleners, rushed at the remnants of the first line of the enemy, went through it as though it were made of pasteboard, and put them to utter rout.

This Russian Horse in less than five minutes after it met our dragoons was flying with all its speed before a force certainly not half its strength. A cheer burst from every lip - in the enthusiasm, officers and men took off their caps and shouted with delight; and thus keeping up the scenic character of their position, they clapped their hands again and again. Lord Raglan at once despatched Lieutenant Curzon, aide-de-camp, to convey his congratulations to Brigadier-General Scarlett, and to say "Well done!" The gallant old officer's face beamed with pleasure when he received the message. " I beg to thank his lordship very sincerely," was his reply. The cavalry did not long pursue their enemy. Their loss was very slight, about thirty-five killed and wounded in both affairs. There were not more than four or five men killed outright, and our most material loss was from the cannon playing on our Heavy Dragoons afterwards, when covering the retreat of our Light Cavalry.

At ten o'clock the Guards and Highlanders of the First Division were seen moving towards the plains from their camp. The Duke of Cambridge came up to Lord Raglan for orders, and his Lordship, ready to give the honour of the day to Sir Colin Campbell, who commanded at Balaklava, told his Royal Highness to place himself under the direction of the Brigadier. At forty minutes after ten, the Fourth Division also took up their position in advance of Balaklava. The cavalry were then on the left front of our position, facing the enemy; the Light Cavalry Brigade was on the left flank forward; the Heavy Cavalry Brigade en echelon in reserve, with guns, on the right; the 4th Royal Irish, the 5th Dragoon Guards, and Greys, on the left of the brigade, the Enniskillens and 1st Royals on the right. The Fourth Division took up ground in the centre; the Guards and Highlanders filed off towards the extreme right, and faced the redoubts, from which the Russians opened on them with artillery, which was silenced by the rifle skirmishers under Lieut. Godfrey, and, after a time, retired.

At fifty minutes after ten, General Canrobert, attended by his staff, and Brigadier-General Rose, rode up to Lord Raglan and the staffs of the two Generals and their escorts mingled together in praise of the magnificent charge of our cavalry, while the chiefs apart conversed over the operations of the day, which promised to be one of battle. The Russian cavalry, followed by our shot, had retired in confusion, leaving the ground covered with horses and men. At fifty-five minutes after ten, a body of cavalry, the Chasseurs d'Afrique, passed down to the plain, and were loudly cheered by our men. They took up ground in advance of the ridges on our left.

Soon after occurred the glorious catastrophe which filled us all with sorrow. It appeared that the Quartermaster-General, Brigadier Airey, thinking that the Light Cavalry had not gone far enough in front when the enemy's horse had fled, gave an order in writing to Captain Nolan, 15th Hussars, to take to Lord Lucan, directing his Lordship "to advance" his cavalry nearer to the enemy. A braver soldier than Captain Nolan the army did not possess. He was known to all his arm of the service for his entire devotion to his profession, and his name must be familiar to all who take interest in our cavalry for his excellent work on our drill and system of remount and breaking horses. I had the pleasure of his acquaintance, and I know he entertained the most exalted opinions respecting the capabilities of the English horse soldier. Properly led, the British Hussar and Dragoon could in his mind break square, take batteries, ride over columns of infantry, and pierce any other cavalry in the world as if they were made of straw. He thought they had not had the opportunity of doing all that was in their power, and that they had missed even such chances as had been offered to them - that, in fact, they were in some measure disgraced. A matchless horseman and a first-rate swordsman he held in contempt, I am afraid, even grape and canister. He rode off with his orders to Lord Lucan. He is now dead and gone. God forbid I should cast a shade on the brightness of his honour, but I am bound to state what I am told occurred when he reached his Lordship. I should premise that as the Russian cavalry retired, their infantry fell back towards the head of the valley, leaving men in three of the redoubts they had taken, and abandoning the others. They had also placed some guns on the heights over their position on the left of the gorge. Their cavalry joined the reserves, and drew up in six solid divisions, in an oblique line, across the entrance to the gorge. Six battalions of infantry were placed behind them, and about 30 guns were drawn up in front and on the flanks, while masses of infantry were also collected on the hills behind the redoubts on our right. Our cavalry had moved up to the ridge across the valley, on our left, as the ground was broken in front, and had halted in the order I have already mentioned. When Lord Lucan received the order from Captain Nolan, and had read it, he asked, we are told, "Where are we to advance to?" Captain Nolan pointed with his finger to the line of the Russians, and said, "There are the enemy, and there are the guns," or words to that effect, according to the statements made after his death.

It must be premised that Lord Raglan had in the morning only ordered Lord Lucan to move from the position he had taken near the centre redoubt to "the left of the second line of redoubts occupied by the Turks". Seeing that the 93rd and invalids were cut off from the aid of the cavalry, Lord Raglan sent another order to Lord Lucan to send his heavy horse towards Balaklava, and that officer was executing it just as the Russian horse came over the ridge. The Heavy Cavalry charge took place, and the men dismounted on the scene of it. After an interval of half an hour, Lord Raglan again sent an order to Lord Lucan - "Cavalry to advance and take advantage of any opportunity to recover the heights. They will be supported by infantry, which has been ordered to advance upon two fronts."

Lord Raglan's reading of this order is, that the infantry had been ordered to advance on two fronts; but no such interpretation is borne out by the wording of the order. It does not appear either that the infantry had received orders to advance, for the Duke of Cambridge and Sir G. Cathcart state they were not in receipt of such instruction. Lord Lucan advanced his cavalry, however, to the ridge, close to No. 5 redoubt, and while there received from Captain Nolan an order, which is verbatim, as follows "Lord Raglan wishes the cavalry to advance rapidly to the front, follow the enemy, and try to prevent the enemy carrying away the guns; troops of Horse Artillery may accompany. French cavalry is on your left. Immediate."

Lord Lucan, with reluctance, gave the order to Lord Cardigan to advance upon the guns, conceiving that his orders compelled him to do so. The noble Earl, though he did not shrink, also saw the fearful odds against him. Don Quixote in his tilt against the windmill was not near so rash and reckless as the gallant fellows who prepared without a thought to rush on to almost certain death. It is a maxim of war, that " cavalry never act without a support", that "infantry should be close at hand when cavalry carry guns, as the effect is only instantaneous", and that it is necessary to have on the flank of a line of cavalry some squadrons in column, the attack on the flank being most dangerous. The only support our light cavalry had was the reserve of heavy cavalry at a great distance behind them, the infantry and guns being far in the rear. There were no squadrons in column at all, and there was a plain to charge over, before the enemy's guns could be reached, of a mile and a half in length.

At ten minutes past eleven our Light Cavalry Brigade advanced. The whole Brigade scarcely made one effective regiment, according to the numbers of continental armies; and yet it was more than we could spare. As they rushed towards the front, the Russians opened on them from the guns in the redoubt on the right, with volleys of musketry and rifles. They swept proudly past, glittering in the morning sun in all the pride and splendour of war. We could scarcely believe the evidence of our senses! Surely that handful of men were not going to charge an army in position? Alas! it was but too true - their desperate valour knew no bounds, and far indeed was it removed from its so-called better part - discretion. They advanced in two lines, quickening their pace as they closed towards the enemy. A more fearful spectacle was never witnessed than by those who, without the power to aid, beheld their heroic countrymen rushing to the arms of death. At the distance of 1200 yards the whole line of the enemy belched forth, from thirty iron mouths, a flood of smoke and flame, through which hissed the deadly balls. Their flight was marked by instant gaps in our ranks, by dead men and horses, by steeds flying wounded or riderless across the plain. The first line was broken - it was joined by the second, they never halted or checked their speed an instant. With diminished ranks, thinned by those thirty guns, which the Russians had laid with the most deadly accuracy, with a halo of flashing steel above their heads, and with a cheer which was many a noble fellow's death-cry, they flew into the smoke of the batteries; but ere they were lost from view, the plain was strewed with their bodies and with the carcases of horses. They were exposed to an oblique fire from the batteries on the hills on both sides, as well as to a direct fire of musketry.

Through the clouds of smoke we could see their sabres flashing as they rode up to the guns and dashed between them, cutting down the gunners as they stood. We saw them riding through the guns, as I have said; to our delight we saw them returning, after breaking through a column of Russian infantry, and scattering them like chaff, when the flank fire of the battery on the hill swept them down, scattered and broken as they were. Wounded men and dismounted troopers flying towards us told the sad tale - demi-gods could not have done what they had failed to do. At the very moment when they were about to retreat, a regiment of Lancers was hurled upon their flank. Colonel Shewell, of the 8th Hussars, whose attention was drawn to them by Lieutenant Phillips, saw the danger, and rode his few men straight at them, cutting his way through with fearful loss. The other regiments turned and engaged in a desperate encounter. With courage too great almost for credence, they were breaking their way through the columns which enveloped them, when there took place an act of atrocity without parallel in the modern warfare of civilized nations. The Russian gunners, when the storm of cavalry passed, returned to their guns, and poured murderous volleys of grape and canister on the mass of struggling men and horses. It was as much as our Heavy Cavalry Brigade could do to cover the retreat of the miserable remnants of that band of heroes as they returned to the place they had so lately quitted in all the pride of life. At thirty-five minutes past eleven not a British soldier, except the dead and dying, was left in front of these bloody Muscovite guns.

From The British Expedition to the Crimea by W. H. Russell (G. Routledge, 1858)

THE ROYAL SAPPERS AND MINERS AT SEBASTOPOL

No time was lost in making the most of the position won by the gallantry of the besiegers; but on the 8th June, owing to the exhausted state of the troops from the labours of the previous night, no working party could be provided for the right attack. Fifty-two sappers, however, took their places as usual in the lines, repairing embrasures, improving the cover of the quarries, and deepening the communications to them. To preserve their energies, they were employed in four reliefs of four hours each throughout the day. Very heavy was the firing from the Russian batteries during the first relief, occasioning many casualties among the guard of the trenches and harassing though not interrupting the workmen. On the left there were 150 linesmen and 38 sappers scattered over the trenches, restoring demolished embrasures and parapets, and re-roofing magazines torn up by shells.

While thus employed in No. 10 battery, situated on a central projection of the second parallel, second-corporal James Fraser - a fearless young non-commissioned officer - was killed. Fraser was working in an embrasure - a mere crag, so complete was its disruption - patching up the left cheek with sandbags, while corporal McEachern was reconstructing the right one. The firing on the battery was fierce, but the two corporals, stript to their trousers and shirts, toiled away with dauntless perseverance. "Never mind the rascals," said Fraser, with an encouraging smile, " we'll finish it in spite of them." Such was his determination; but a few moments after, he was blown from the embrasure by a round shot, which carried away his right arm and the whole of his breast and ribs, exposing his quivering heart. McEachern heard the shot pass and felt the heat which its velocity imparted; and on turning round to see how his comrade had fared, he saw him doubled up on a pile of projectiles and the gunners and workmen gathering up his remains. McEachern had seen too many such catastrophes to slacken his energies, and so resuming the work as if nothing had happened he left it only when the cheeks were finished.

Private John Malcolm, an hour after, was sent into the same embrasure to clear the sole, as the gun in its rear could not be sufficiently depressed to fire with advantage. Stripped to the work, he was shovelling away the debris, when a splinter from a shell struck him severely on the head. At the instant, he fell from the aperture to the platform, and the next moment a shower of fierce stones fell on him, fretting his flannel shirt as if a rasp had torn it up and wounding him in both shoulders. In the night following there were 59 sappers in the front, who were succeeded next morning by 71 men. Many laboured at the different batteries and privates John Sykes and William Orr, in charge of No. 1 o battery, left attack, were named to Lord Raglan as having behaved with conspicuous zeal and coolness in removing the debris of broken gabions and split-bags from the disfigured embrasures and rebuilding the cheeks. So heavy was the fire at the time, that one gun was disabled in the battery and some of the artillery carriages injured. General Jones was an eye-witness of the manly way in which Orr entered the embrasures between the rounds of fire, and of his unruffled exertions to clear the soles and mend the revetments; and when the general had it in his power to mark, in a substantial manner, his appreciation of the private's intrepid demeanour, he obtained for him "a distinguished service" medal and a gratuity of five pounds.

By the 10th June, on which date there were 94 sappers in the front, the batteries were all in admirable order, another screen overlooking the Woronzoff road was finished, and the lodgment and its communications looked grim with details which promised to be formidable when completed. On that day, fifty men of the line had been thrown into the quarries to assist in converting them to the besiegers' will; but after a while, so accurate and fierce was the fire upon them from a mortar and a gun on the right of the tower, that the party was necessarily withdrawn. "Whistling Dick", from the mortar alluded to, was doing its best to thin the workmen; but luckily its terrific presence was unaccompanied by any serious disaster. Still the sappers, twelve in number, were retained at this dangerous spot; and working away amid descending shells bursting in all directions and splinters driving even into obscure angles, they strengthened the parapet by building stones into the revetment, made loopholes, and continued the formation of the banquette. At three o'clock in the afternoon, Captain Browne of the engineers, persevering in his endeavours to work the lodgment, sent another fifty men into it who laboured in the quarries till regularly relieved. More than fifty casualties occurred in and about the quarries during the day; among these was private William Lang who was dangerously wounded by a shell which carried away his arm. A group of his comrades, who were near at the time, threw themselves down to avoid its splinters. Awful moments followed, each expecting, but hoping to escape the death that seemed inevitable. Fortunately the shell buried itself in the earth, then fizzed in paroxysms for a few seconds, when, grinding further into the soil, the fuse providentially was smothered. Another sapper, name unknown, was wounded in the left attack. Seventy men of the corps were in the trenches during the night of the 10th scattered over the works of the two attacks. The lodgment, still offering occasion for anxious solicitude, progressed with energy and a new trench was formed on a segmental trace in front of the quarries, taking the captured ambuscade as the base of the figure. The spring of the bow issued from the right of the lodgment, then, bending away in an arch, abutted on the left of the quarries. The trench was clear of the salient of the Redan, but intersected the Malakoff abattis at a point where a gap had recently been made by a round shot from the besiegers. All the gabions, 180 in number, which lined the excavation, were staked and filled before the morning. Not a shot or bullet came in the direction during its progress. Twelve sappers were appointed to this new trench, who, receiving the gabions from the line, placed them on the sweep of the curve with a rapidity and sprightliness so marked, it seemed as if the men were chasing each other to the goal. The workmen were chiefly of the 19th regiment, by whom, and a party from the light division, about 180 in all, the gabions were filled. Next day there were 103 sappers in the lines, and 74 at night. At daybreak on the 12th, there were 81 men in the front. Considerable exertions had been made in mining on the left attack, principally in the round-hill parallel, where, stopped by rock at every step, not a move could be made ahead, till by great bodily exertion, and patient coolness against inevitable personal risks, the obstruction was blown away. Laborious and fatiguing as were these duties, they were executed with no abatement of care; and it may be mentioned that from the first, out of thousands of blasts fired successfully throughout the works, and many more which failed in critical situations, only two accidents by mining had occurred. A more striking proof of the proficiency of the men need scarcely be adduced. The sufferers were private John Stancombe who lost the sight of one of his eyes, and lance-corporal William Eastley who was severely wounded by a stone of about 14 pounds striking him in the back. The former was blown up, and receiving the blast full in his face, blood poured from a hundred punctures, and when the wounds were healed his skin was thickly speckled with blue marks as if elaborately tattooed by some unskilful mariner.

After an attack — when other soldiers are snatching a few hours' sleep - the sappers are at work as usual.

Who will dare stand among the ruins? Here comes a sapper followed by another from behind a traverse to survey the desolation. Well is it that night approaches to cover the adventure. It is more than dusk already. Into the breach they vault with fluttering hearts, for no panoply guards them; no helmet, no cuirass, protects them. Soon the emotion passes and the calmness of extremity prepares them for the worst. Each has his cap pressed down on his brow, and his greatcoat - pegged or pinned in front, with perhaps a solitary button to connect the breasts - is girdled with a couple of well-worn belchers or a piece of cordage. Removing the debris, they build up the faces with fresh material handed to them by some constant linesmen. Now a gabion is fixed and others are forced into position in quick succession. Sand-bags are crushed into the baskets till they creak, and others, laid in row, crown the work. Care is taken to give the necessary slopes to the cheeks to prevent them tumbling down. All the interstices and crests are made solid with rammed earth and bags, and not a nook or chink occurs but something is found to jam into it to make it whole. Upon the merlon* toils another sapper strengthening it with stones and earth handed to him by his assistants in the battery. Perspiration drops like rain over his beard, and, driven by his strong energy through every pore, moistens the rags which cover him from the night damp. Some bales of hides being brought, feeling makes up for the want of vision in so dark a night, and the cheeks are at length covered with hairy skins. Prudence has adapted their use as well to aid in preserving the embrasures, as to save them from flaming during the rapidity of our own fire. Now the sole of the opening is being improved and sloped. Up to the front the comrades push. So far are they away you scarce can see them. Deadly missiles fly onward and around and Minie bullets with a wheezing noise spend their force in the parapet. Who's touched? Neither. One however has had a ball through his cap. Still on they work with strength somewhat abated, but no deterioration of spirit, till a couple of gabions, struck behind by a shell, are forced outwards and knock down the operators. The fall of one is awkward, for his head overhangs the trench and the shelving slope of the sole threatens to shoot him headlong into the ditch. Catching at a stake he breaks his descent and wriggling back into the aperture, crawls to the spot where his exertions were interrupted. Joined by his comrade just rising from beneath a pile of broken sand-bags they recommence the restoration. Fair excuse this for suspending the work but un-dismayed they persevere. Eventually their toils end; their work is completed; and after six hours' exposure, they quit the scene uninjured. It is otherwise in the next embrasure, for one is mown down by a shot and the other badly wounded. Such is the fortune of war.

*The higher portion of the parapet was the merlon; the gap through which the gun was fired was the embrasure.

From A History of the Royal Sappers and Miners by T. J. Connolly (Longman, Brown, Green, Longmans and Roberts, 1857)

THE NAVAL BRIGADE AT THE REDAN

Midshipman Evelyn Wood was with the leading ladder party:

It is difficult to describe adequately the intensity of the fire. Various kinds of projectiles cut up the ground all around us, but not continuously in their fullest force, for while there was no cessation of the shower of missiles, which pattered on the ground like tropical rain when the monsoon breaks, at times there were death-dealing gusts of increased density, which swept down the hill, felling our men as a reaping-machine levels standing crops.

Captain Peel, standing on the parapet waving his sword in the dim light, cheered on our men, shouting, "Come on, sailors; don't let the soldiers beat you." At this appeal the whole of the ladder party, some of whom had taken cover at the first outburst of the Russian fire, ran forward at a steady double, simultaneously with the skirmishers and wool-bag carriers. The skirmishers had started 50 yards in front of us, and went straight up to the abatis, where I was speaking to one of the leaders when he was mortally wounded. Although Daniels and I had previously determined to remain with Captain Peel, from the moment we started I lost sight of both my friends.

When I was riding down to the battery, I felt so weak as to be incapable of fighting hand to hand even a boy of my own size, for I had been living on tinned milk and rice for over a week, and I instinctively realised the value of Michael Hardy, who was holding me on my pony, as a fighting man. Thinking I would secure at all events the support of one strong arm, I said, "Hardy, when we go out I shall stick to the Captain, and you must stick to me." Hardy replied, somewhat evasively, "Yes, I will stick to him if he goes well to the front;" and this indomitable Irishman carried out his resolve, and permitted no one to surpass him in the Assault.

Now invigorated by excitement, I ran forward in front of the ladder parties. Before we had gone 100 yards, several sailors were struck down, and I was hit by a bullet while cheering on the Bluejackets and waving my sword, which was knocked five yards away from me. My arm was paralysed by the jar, and I thought it was off, as I instinctively dropped on one knee. On looking down, I saw it was only a flesh wound of the hand, and jumped up hastily, fearing that anyone passing might think I was skulking. Picking up my sword, I found it was twisted like a cork-screw, so threw it down, and with it the scabbard, which had got between my legs. I had no pistol, and thus was without any weapon, but that did not occur to my mind as I ran on to overtake the leading ladder. Before I had rejoined it, my comrades had suffered considerably; the senior Lieutenant had been slightly wounded, and Dalyell had lost his left arm, shattered by grape-shot.

Captain Peel was hit, when half-way up the glacis,* by a bullet which passed through his left arm. He became faint, and was accompanied back by Mr. Daniels, who was the only unwounded officer out of the seven who went out with the Right ladder party. He escaped injury, but his pistol-case was shot through in two places, and his clothes were cut by several bullets. Thus, within about 250 yards, or about half the distance to be passed over, I was the only Naval officer remaining effective. It was possible that I unconsciously brought up my left shoulder to avoid the fire from the Redan; but anyhow, having no weight to carry, I again outstripped the leading ladder men, and then retraced my steps for 100 yards, although unwillingly, for I was intensely anxious to reach Redan, although with no clear idea what to do when I got there.

* The slope in front of the wall.

We started with ten ladders, but there were only four being carried forward when I rejoined my party; and I could see none of those entrusted to the soldiers, although there were some few men still struggling forward with wool bags.

If any of my younger comrades in either Service have to undertake a similar task, I recommend them to put an officer with every ladder.

With the four ladders carried by sailors, with whom the Petty officers had replaced as carriers men who had been killed, we instinctively inclined to our right hand to avoid the storm of missiles from two guns on the (proper) left face of the Redan, but after advancing another 60 yards came under fire of guns placed in the curtain connecting the left of the Redan with the middle ravine near the dockyard, and these caused us to bring up our right shoulders.

In the Siege-work plans made by our Royal Engineers the abatis is shown as standing 100 yards from the counter scarp, or outside edge of the ditch. Doubtless it was so after the 8th September, but on the 18th June it was certainly 20 yards nearer, and in places - for it did not run in a straight line - even closer. When I reached it, 50 yards on the Malakoff side of the Salient, I had with me only two ladders; these were carried by four and three men respectively, and I was in front of the leading ladder.

Its carriers were reduced to three, and then the right-hand man falling, I took his place. The second ladder now fell to the ground, the men being killed or wounded by a blast of case-shot, and when we were 25 yards from the abatis my ladder carriers were reduced to two. The man in front was only a few years older than myself, an Ordinary seaman, but he had shown no other feeling than the desire to be first up. I had not carried it far when the man alongside of me was killed, and then the Ordinary seaman in front, feeling no doubt he was bearing an undue share of the weight, not knowing I was under the ladder, turning his head as far as he could, addressed me as his messmate.

"Come along, Bill; let's get our beggar up first." Before he recognised me, while his face was still turned backwards, he was killed, and with him tumbled the ladder.

In my heart I experienced a sense of relief, from the feeling that my responsibility was over, as even my most gallant Chief, William Peel, would not expect me to carry a ladder 18 feet in length by myself. It was now lying within 30 yards of the abatis, under the slight shelter of which a few scattered soldiers were crouching: some were firing, a great many shouting, while on the parapet 15 feet above us stood Russians four and in places six deep, firing at, and calling on us sarcastically to walk in. I looked round, and at once saw there was no chance of our accepting the invitation. The abatis where I was standing, between 60 and 70 yards from the salient, was a strong fence 4 feet thick, and 5 feet high in places, made up of stout trees, and beams from 6 to 8 inches in diameter, closed with brushwood. There were places where a man could have squeezed through the holes made by our shells, but only one at a time, and even then, assuming that he crossed unscathed the open space intervening between the abatis and the ditch, there was still a more formidable obstacle. From the bottom of the ditch the top of the parapet on which the Russians were standing was 26 feet high.

The Storming party had dwindled down to 100, and I perceived at once that unless heavy reinforcements came up there was no chance of carrying the work. While looking round to count heads, Lieutenant Graves of the Royal Engineers asked me if I had seen Captain Peel. I said ' No, not since we crossed the parapet,' and as he passed on, he was killed. He spoke as calmly as when, repairing the embrasure on the 10th April, a round-shot cut the ground from under his feet. Now an officer detaching a bough from the abatis waved it over his head, and cheerily called on the men to follow him, but while shouting he was pierced by several bullets, and fell lifeless, I was greatly impressed by the courage of a young Sergeant, who was trying to collect men to accompany him through or over the abatis. After calling in vain on those immediately to follow him, he lost his temper, and shouted, "I'll tell my right-hand man to follow me, and if he fails I'll shoot him." He brought his rifle down to the "Ready ", and said, "Private —, will you follow me?" I was almost touching them, and seeing by the Sergeant's eye that he was in earnest, stood for a few seconds studying the determined look on the man's face. The Private looked deliberately on the hundreds of Russians above us, and then ran his eye right and left of where we were standing, as if estimating the number of his comrades, who certainly did not exceed 100, and with as much determination as the Sergeant said, "No, I won't." The non-commissioned officer threw his rifle to his shoulder with the intention of carrying out his threat, but in doing so, struck by a grape-shot, he fell dead.

I now dropped on one knee to talk to an officer sitting under the abatis as to our chances of getting in, when he was hit just above the waist-belt by a bullet. He tossed about in great pain, calling on the Almighty. I was somewhat perturbed, but had seen too many men killed to be seriously affected, until he apostrophised his mother; this allusion distressed me so much that I rose, and walked slowly in the direction of the Malakoff, looking to see if there were any weaker spots in the abatis. I had only gone a few yards, when glancing upwards I saw a section of Russians 'following ' me with their muskets. Instinctively throwing up my left arm to shield my face, I was walking on, when a gun was fired with case-shot close to me. The missiles came crashing through the abatis, and one weighing 5½ oz. struck my arm just below the funny-bone. This sent me screaming to the ground, and I rolled some yards down the slope of the hill, where I lay insensible.

I do not know how long I was unconscious, but it cannot have been many minutes; for the whole affair did not last more than half an hour. I was aroused by an Irish corporal, who shook my arm, saying, " Matey,* if you are going on, you had better go at once, or you'll get bagoneted."** I presume it was the pain in my arm which brought me back to consciousness, but I answered the man with an outburst of bad language. He drew himself erect, and bringing his hand across his body to the rifle said, "I beg your pardon, sir, I did not know you were an officer. Can I help you?" "Yes, help me up, but by the other hand." He then told me the "Retire" had been sounded some minutes earlier, and that all our people were going back. In spite of the number of men firing at us at less than 100 yards' distance, he helped me up carefully, taking care not to hurt my arm, and then bending down his head, ran as hard as he could towards our trenches. I followed him towards the 8-gun battery, but very slowly; for although I had not previously felt my weakness since the moment we crossed the trenches to assault, I had now become faint, and could walk only slowly, although grape and case shot fell thickly around me.

As I rolled down the slope my wounded arm, probably from instinct, remained uppermost. There was nothing to indicate I was an officer, for I had thrown away my scabbard when my sword was destroyed; my gold band cap was underneath me, and my blue serge jacket was threadbare and dirty.
** Bayoneted

When I had gone 300 yards, I saw several men running with their heads bent down along a ditch, made direct towards the Redan for about 100 yards beyond the Quarries, during the last few nights. It was only two feet deep, but with the rank grass three feet high on the slope, gave slight shelter from view. I had walked only a few yards in the ditch, however, when the screams of wounded men, who had crawled in for shelter, and were now hurt by the soldiers running over them, caused me to get out and walk away. I had scarcely left the ditch when it was swept by case-shot from three guns in succession, and most of the men who had been running over their comrades fell killed or wounded on top of them. As I approached the trenches in front of our 3rd parallel, from which we had started, the last of the Covering party which had remained out to fire on the Russians, were returning inside the trenches. I made for a place where the slight bank was worn down, in order to avoid the increased exertion of mounting up four feet, when a young soldier passed me on my left side, and doubtless not noticing I was wounded knocked me heavily on the arm, saying, " Move on, please." As he crossed the parapet, I caught the butt of the rifle to pull myself up, and he turned his face, saying "What are you doing?" A round-shot passing over my right shoulder struck him between the shoulders, and I stepped over the remains of his body so exhausted as to be indifferent to his death and to my preservation, due to his rudeness in jostling me out of my turn at the gap.

On the safe side of this little parapet, there sat a sailor who made me feel ashamed of my own powers of endurance. He had been severely wounded in the right hand, and had lost two of his fingers, and thinking how helpless I had become, I stood still to admire the man's coolness and self-possession. With his left hand he had pulled out of his trousers the tail of his shirt, and holding it in his teeth, had torn off nearly three strips when I approached. With these he was bandaging up his hand in a manner which would have done credit to a class who had gone through "First Aid to the Wounded", and he answered my question as to his wound quite cheerily.

When I reached the foot of the parapet of the 8-gun battery I was unable to walk up it, and fell to the ground at the first attempt. When I did surmount it, I hesitated to step down to the banquette, fearing to jar my arm, and paused so long that a sergeant, probably not wanting to see more fire drawn on to the spot, called out, "Jump, jump, you little devil, or you will get killed." I consigned him to a hot place, and sank down where I was, when two officers seeing my state came out and carried me inside the work.

I was taken to a doctor (an Irishman) whom I had known for some time, and was greeted warmly with the exclamation, "Sit down, my dear boy, an' I'll have your arm off before you know where you are." I steadily but with some difficulty evaded his kind intention, and was eventually put into a stretcher and carried to camp by four Bluejackets. As we left the battery the stretcher-bearers and I had an escape, for a shell burst just in front of us, cutting up the ground between the fore and rear carriers, who, however, did not flinch; but as we passed through the camp of the 4th Division, as they changed arms, the iron hook which kept the stretcher apart unshipped, and I fell heavily to the ground on my wounded arm.

While waiting in the operating-tent for my turn for the table, I was interested by the extraordinary fortitude of a Bluejacket, who discussed the morning's failure without a break in his voice while the doctors were removing two of his fingers at the third joint. When my turn came, I had a heated argument with the surgeons, who wished to amputate the arm above the elbow. The Navy had then an officer dangerously ill from a wound received a few days earlier, in which case amputation had been delayed too long, and all but the senior Doctor wished to take off my arm. To him I appealed to be allowed the chance, and to persuade him I underwent considerable pain. The eight who were for removing the limb declared that it was impossible that any use could be obtained from the arm, the elbow-joint of which had been shattered. To prove that it was not, I doubling my fist raised the arm as high as I could, until the case-shot met the fore and upper arm, on which the senior Medical officer decided that he would at all events try to save the limb.

From Midshipman to Field Marshal by Sir Evelyn Wood, FM, VC (Methuen and Co., 1906)

Chapter 3

The Last Eleven at Maiwand

In 1880 Britain was involved in a war with Afghanistan, not for the first nor the last time. Through a series of miscalculations a small force of British and Indians at Maiwand found themselves confronted by an army outnumbering them ten to one. Furthermore the Afghan army had powerful artillery. The result was a defeat for the British force but it went into history as the scene of the stand of the 'last eleven' at Maiwand. The eleven were all that remained of the 66th Foot, the Royal Berkshire Regiment, a total of eight, and the survivors of other spirited actions, three in number; Major Blackwood, a Gunner, Lt Hinde, a Grenadier, and Lt T. R. Henn of the Royal Engineers. Earlier in the day Henn had led a desperate resistance of the Sappers in which hand- to-hand fighting had been conducted with whatever weapons came to hand. Not until every one of the last eleven was wounded did the Afghans dare advance to finish them off. This in itself was an exceptional even if unintended tribute from a people as brave as the Afghans. (A later member of Henn's family, Brigadier T. R. Henn, CBE, was on the SHAEF staff which planned the D-day landings in 1944.)

As the mutinous troops had plundered the stores of supplies collected at Girishk by Shere Ali Khan, and as reports reached Colonel St. John that it was Ayub Khan's intention, if he were to cross the Halmand at all, to do so at a point to the north of Girishk, General Burrows determined to abandon the position he had hitherto occupied, and retire to Khushki-i-Nakhud, distant thirty miles from Girishk and forty-five from Kandahar, where several roads from the Halmand to Kandahar converge, and where supplies were plentiful. This retirement was effected during the night of the 15th, and on the morning of the 16th the troops occupied their old camping-ground. On the 18th a more favourable site, two miles nearer Mir-Karez, was selected, the stores being collected in an enclosure, and arrangements made to leave the baggage with a small guard, should it be necessary to move out to meet the enemy. This camp was held till the morning of the 27th of July. Reliable information concerning Ayub's movements was meagre in the extreme, and was mainly derived from spies sent out by Colonel St. John, under the auspices of Shere Ali Khan; for some days little was ascertained beyond the bare fact that Ayub had reached the Halmand, and moving from Girishk, had distributed his troops along the river bed, south of the ford of Haidarabad. Cavalry patrols were sent out daily, but nothing of the enemy was seen until the 21st. On that day a reconnoitring party encountered a small force at Sangbar, a village situated about midway between Khushki-i-Nakhud and Girishk, and after exchanging a few shots, retired. On the 22nd, Sangbar was again found to be occupied, and the following day a reconnaissance in force towards that place found about 600 of Ayub's horsemen in the plain below the Garmao hills. Shortly afterwards the enemy retired, pursued by the cavalry and shelled by the horse-artillery guns at long ranges for some miles.

During this period the brigade received some small accessions to its strength from Kandahar, and General Burrows was kept fully advised by General Primrose of the instructions which were being transmitted to him from Army Headquarters. The most important of these was contained in a communication despatched from Simla on the 21st of July, by which General Burrows was given full liberty to attack Ayub in the event of his considering himself strong enough to do so, and by which he was informed that Government considered it of the greatest political importance that Ayub's force should be dispersed, and prevented from passing on to Ghazni.

Vague reports daily found their way into camp concerning the strength of the enemy; the regular troops, however, were believed to number 4,000 cavalry, and 4,000 to 5,000 infantry, and to have at their disposal thirty guns. In addition to these there were the deserters from the Wali's army, another 2,000, besides an irregular force composed of malcontents from all the unsettled districts of the Halmand. Of the number of the latter it was impossible to form any estimate. At Kandahar at this time, great uneasiness prevailed in the city, and large numbers of families were leaving daily, ostensibly for fear of Ayub's approach.

On the afternoon of the 26th of July important information reached camp at Khushki-i-Nakhud. 2,000 of the enemy's cavalry and a large number of Ghazis, it was reported, had arrived at Garmao and Maiwand, and were to be followed immediately by Ayub Khan with the main body of his army, his intention being, it was said, to make his way into the Argandab Valley by the Maiwand Pass. It thus became necessary, in order to carry out the directions which had been received with reference to preventing him from slipping past towards Ghazni, to arrest his further progress without delay; and it was believed that by a rapid advance on the village of Maiwand his force might be cut in two; and his advanced cavalry at Garmao driven to the northward before aid could reach it.

At 6.30 a.m. on the 27th of July camp was struck, and the brigade - now consisting of E/B, R.H.A., the smooth-bore battery captured from the mutineers, 516 of all ranks of the 66th Foot, 316 of the 3rd Light Cavalry, 260 of the 3rd Sind Horse, 45 of the Sappers and Miners, 648 of the 1st Grenadiers, and 625 of Jacob's Rifles, in all 2,599 of ranks and arms, inclusive of 34 Europeans and 50 natives in hospital - commenced its march on Maiwand. The hostile state of the country rendered it impossible to leave anything behind in safety, and the column was consequently encumbered by an enormous quantity of ordnance and commissariat stores and baggage.

The advance lay through a belt of cultivated land, along the right bank of the Khushki-i-Nakhud river, which was at this season perfectly dry. At 8 a.m. the village of Mushak was reached and a halt was made to allow the baggage to close up. Half an hour later a move was made to Karezak, eight miles distant from the Khushki-i-Nakhud camp, and four miles south-east of Maiwand. Here it was reported that Ayub Khan's whole army, including his artillery, was in the immediate vicinity, and marching on Maiwand; but the information which had been recently derived from native sources had proved so untrustworthy, that little heed was given to the rumour. About 10 a.m., however, a brief reconnaissance disclosed large masses of the enemy's cavalry moving across the left front towards Maiwand. As the brigade continued to advance, these bodies were observed to incline in a northerly direction towards Garmao. A thick haze which shrouded the surrounding country precluded the possibility, however, of forming any correct estimate of their disposition and numbers.

About 10 a.m. the advanced cavalry occupied without opposition the village of Mundabad, three miles to the south-west of Maiwand, it being General Burrows' intention to avail himself of the walled enclosures of the village for relieving the brigade of the heavy baggage train with which it was encumbered, and then to make his dispositions for attacking the enemy. While the arrival of the baggage was awaited, General Nuttall proceeded with two of the guns of E/B, R.H.A., under Major Blackwood, to reconnoitre the enemy's position from the edge of a broad and deep ravine, running north and south, in front of the village.

To the west of Mundabad, and separated from the village by the ravine already alluded to, stretched a waterless stony plain, bounded on its northern and north-western extremity by three parallel ranges of hills, which, extending in a north-easterly direction, enclose between them the Garmao and Maiwand Valleys. Beyond, and opening into the Maiwand Valley - the more easterly of the two - is the Khakrez Valley, through the eastern barrier of which, north of the Maiwand Pass, are roads leading towards Kandahar and the Upper Argandab. It was across this stony plain to the westward that Ayub Khan's army, almost entirely hidden from view by the dense haze, was moving in an easterly direction towards the village of Maiwand, which, lying a little to the west of the pass of the same name, covers its entrance as well as the approaches to the valuable water-supply in that neighbourhood. Had General Burrows desired to remain on the defensive, the position he now occupied offered many advantages. The village of Mundabad would have afforded protection for the baggage; a number of low walled enclosures which connected its various parts would have given admirable cover for the infantry; and there was an abundance of water. But acting under the erroneous impression that the enemy had no guns, and that their force, whatever its strength might be, would very possibly retire without risking an encounter, General Burrows considered that a favourable opportunity had arrived for taking the initiative, and determined on delivering an attack without further delay.

An incident now occurred which at once precipitated the commencement of the action. While General Nuttall and Major Blackwood were observing the movements of groups of the enemy who were visible from the edge of the broad nullah, two of the four advanced guns of E/B, R.H.A. under the command of Lieut. Maclaine, escorted by a troop of the 3rd Sind Horse under Lieut. Monteith, had crossed the ravine somewhat lower down, and advancing rapidly across the plain on the extreme left opened fire at a range of 1,800 yards on a large mass of Afghan horsemen who had just become visible. Failing in his attempts to recall this detachment before the guns had entered into action, General Nuttall sent back orders for two guns of the same battery, under Lieut. Osborne, which were with the rear-guard, to hasten up to the front, and crossing the ravine with the 3rd Sind Horse, and Blackwood's two remaining guns, advanced to within 800 yards of the position which had been taken up by Lieut. Maclaine. Here a halt was made to await the arrival of the infantry, Maclaine being at the same time directed to move down nearer the main body.

In the meantime the infantry under General Burrows, with the smooth-bore guns under Captain Slade, had crossed the nullah and deployed in the following order the 66th Foot on the right, the smooth-bore guns in the centre, the 1st Grenadiers on the left, and the 30th Native Infantry (Jacob's Rifles), with the Sappers, in support. Immediately on the left of the infantry line were the four guns of E/B, R.H.A., under Major Blackwood and Lieut. Osborne, supported by 130 sabres of the 3rd Light Cavalry under Major Currie, who, with Captain Mayne of that regiment, also watched the right flank; the two remaining guns of E/B, R.H.A., under Lieut. Maclaine, supported by a troop of the 3rd Sind Horse, were on the extreme left; and in rear, echeloned outside the guns, but with its left thrown back, was a troop of the 3rd Light Cavalry under Lieut. Reid, formed thus to watch a large body of the enemy's cavalry who were threatening the British left flank. Protecting the baggage, which had followed in rear at an interval of about 1,000 yards, were Colonel Malcolm- son and Lieut.

Geoghegan, the former with 96 sabres 3rd Sind Horse, and the latter with 50 sabres 3rd Light Cavalry.

By the time this disposition was effected, the enemy had assumed more definite formations, but nothing had yet occurred to unmask their real strength. Their numbers, however, rapidly developed, and in a short time an advance was made by a large number of Ghazis from the direction of Maiwand upon the British right flank. To meet this movement, the right of the infantry line (the 66th Foot) was thrown back, and the front extended by ordering up two companies of Jacob's Rifles to the extreme left, and filling the gap between the guns and the 66th with the other four companies of Jacob's Rifles and the little party of Sappers. Two of the smooth-bore guns were at the same time withdrawn from the centre to the right, while Lieut. Maclaine, recalled from the extreme left, formed up in the centre with the other four guns of E/B, R.H.A. The whole of the fighting strength was thus in line, ten of the twelve guns being massed in the centre, and two on the extreme right. For the first half-hour the enemy's artillery had made no sign, but by degrees battery after battery was unmasked, till eventually the fire of thirty guns was concentrated on the British position. The infantry were ordered to lie down, but there was little or no cover for the artillery and cavalry; nor could the latter be withdrawn out of range, as it was necessary to demonstrate continuously against the swarm of Afghan horsemen, which from the first began circling round both flanks and threatening the baggage. The Ghazis on the right advanced to within 500 yards of the infantry, but recoiling before the Martini fire of the 66th, sought cover in a small watercourse and remained stationary.

For two hours the artillery duel was continued with little change in the disposition of the British troops, two of the smoothbore guns, under Captain Slade, being temporarily withdrawn to the left, however, to check an advance in that quarter. During this period the numbers of the enemy on either flank were continually augmented and though General Nuttall's force succeeded in preventing the Afghan horsemen establishing themselves in the immediate rear of the British infantry, its strength was totally inadequate to control the more extended flanking operations, and in a short time the brigade was all but surrounded, the rear-guard being hotly engaged in protecting the baggage. By 2 o'clock p.m. the cavalry had lost 14 per cent, of the men in the front line and 149 horses, and though the infantry, lying on the ground, had not suffered so severely, they had not escaped punishment. The day was unusually hot and sultry, and want of water had soon begun to tell upon the Sepoys, who were continually leaving the ranks and falling to the rear to assuage their thirst.

About 2.30 p.m., the smooth-bore guns ran short of ammunition, and a few minutes later were ordered to the rear to replenish. Their withdrawal was followed by a general move along the enemy's front, the Afghan horsemen on the British left spreading out in loose order and endeavouring to complete the cordon around the British troops, the right rear of the column having been already turned by large bodies of mounted and dismounted irregulars, who had taken possession of the village of Mundabad. The fire of the enemy's guns now momentarily slackened, and swarms of Ghazis appeared to be preparing to rush upon the British centre and left. At this critical juncture the two companies of Jacob's Rifles on the extreme left fell back in disorder, the men, who had been suffering severely from want of water, being completely cowed by the heavy artillery fire to which they had been subjected, and the casualties which had occurred in their ranks. Unsteadied by the Rifles, the 1st Grenadiers, which had twice successfully checked the advance of the enemy, also gave way, and a few moments afterwards the collapse on the left flank was complete, the Native Infantry rolling up like a wave towards the right, the Sepoys, surrounded and mixed up with the Ghazis, being swept back on the guns of E/B, R.H.A. A very gallant stand was here made by the artillery, who had throughout borne the brunt of the enemy's fire, the gunners, ably seconded by the little detachment of Sappers under Lieut. Henn, R.E., fighting the Ghazis with handspikes, sponge-rods, and other improvised weapons. When the order to limber up and retire was reluctantly given, there was barely sufficient time to carry it out, and the two guns under Lieut. Maclaine, which occupied a position a little in advance of the rest of the battery, remaining behind to fire one more round, fell into the enemy's hands. The Ghazis now threw the whole of their strength on the retreating Native Infantry, who, in one hopelessly confused mass, were falling back upon the 66th Foot. The havoc which ensued was appalling. Officers and men were carried back by sheer weight of numbers, the Sepoys, making little attempt to defend themselves, in many instances, being literally dragged out of the ranks and massacred. A cavalry charge was now ordered as a last resource to cover the infantry retirement, but cavalry, as well as infantry, were demoralized by the terrible artillery fire to which they had been subjected, and in consequence of a considerable detachment being absent on duty with the baggage in rear, and of many horses having been killed or disabled, General Nuttall had only 255 sabres at his disposal. With these numbers a charge was made in the direction of the captured guns, but not being driven home, it failed, and the troopers retired in disorder. All subsequent attempts made at this time to induce the men to rally were unsuccessful, and the squadrons were withdrawn to the east side of the main ravine immediately in front of the village of Mundabad, where, covered by the horse artillery guns, they again formed up facing the enemy. In the meantime the infantry, hemmed in by the Ghazis on all sides, retired laboriously towards the village of Khig, situated about a mile and a half north-east of Mundabad.

After crossing the ravine the scattered remnants of the Native Infantry streamed away to the eastward. All General Burrows's efforts to rally them were unavailing; discipline was utterly gone, and in spite of every endeavour to induce them to close on the cavalry and artillery, the fugitives persisted in inclining away in a direction which carried them farther and farther from water. A small number had, however, joined a body of the 66th, which, rallying round its colours, made a gallant stand with a small party of the Sappers, in a garden enclosure near Khig. Here, amongst others, several officers of the 66th, including Colonel Galbraith, were killed, and the little force becoming rapidly outflanked, again retired, making stand after stand, until at last only eleven men survived. So valiantly did these eleven bear themselves that it was not till the last man was disabled that the Ghazis dared to advance on them. Amongst this band were Major Blackwood, R.H.A, Lieut. Henn, R.E., and Lieut. Hinde, 1st Grenadiers.

Whilst the infantry was thus hotly engaged in the enclosures of the village of Khig, the cavalry, covered by the guns, and now in proper formation, moved on after the baggage, which was by this time stretching away for miles in the direction of Kandahar. One or more of the enemy's guns opened fire upon this portion of the force, but a single troop was sufficient to hold the irregular horse, who attempted to follow, completely in check. The majority of the men wounded early in the day were at this time well in advance with the smooth-bore battery, but others, less fortunate, had fallen behind, and were picked up and carried on. At 5 p.m. the bed of the Khushk-i-Nakhud river, about four miles from the scene of action, was reached, and the two lines of stragglers effected a junction. The retreat was then continued, a troop of cavalry covering the rear as before, with the aid of the horse artillery guns, the limbers of which were now crowded with wounded. Pursuit had by this time practically ceased, and although groups of the enemy's horse were seen on the opposite side of the river-bed, they were kept at a distance by the fire of the dismounted troopers.

The line of baggage and wounded officers and men formed a straggling column upwards of six miles in length, and were following a route which, after passing within a short distance of the camping-ground previously occupied at Khushk-i-Nakhud, crossed a bare and waterless expanse to Hanz-i-Madat, sixteen miles distant. Shortly before nightfall General Burrows pushed forward with the main body of the cavalry by a divergent route towards Ata Karez for water, and an orderly was sent forward to turn the retreating line in that direction; the rout, however, had become so general, and the remnants of the brigade were so widely scattered, that this was found to be impossible, and the greater number of the fugitives, suffering agonies of thirst, and impelled onward by alarms which were constantly raised that the enemy were in close pursuit, struggled painfully on to Hanz-i- Madat, which was at length reached shortly before midnight. After a long search, a well was found, and water was obtained for the first time after leaving the battle-field. The first care was for the wounded on the guns, and at the end of an hour everyone had drunk. Stragglers were continually coming in, and at once hurried to the water, each succeeding quarter of an hour adding largely to the numbers; happily, however, the noisy gathering, struggling angrily for precedence, was completely unmolested, although the barking of watch-dogs gave warning that a village was not far distant. After half an hour's rest the troops struggled on to Asu Khan, where the cultivated portion of the Argandab was entered, and numerous villages had to be passed through. The news of the defeat had been spread by the retainers of the Wali Shere Ali Khan, who had sought safety in flight from the battle-field early in the day, and as soon as it grew light large numbers of armed villagers, greedy for loot, turned out and harassed the retreat. Hovering around the line, they made dashes wherever a gap occurred, and numbers of followers fell victims to their knives. The troops had to fight, more or less, all the way to Kokaran, from whence a small force under Brigadier-General Brooke, which had been sent to their aid, covered the further retirement to Kandahar, and was instrumental in saving a large number of followers from destruction. Between Asu Khan and Sinjiri, Lieut. Whitby, 1st Grenadiers, was killed, and Lieut. Maclaine, R.H.A., taken prisoner, both officers having been surprised while in search of water. Besides the two horse artillery guns captured by the enemy, five of the smooth-bore guns had to be abandoned, one after the other, during the retreat, four of the horses in one team alone dying of exhaustion. About noon on the 28th the remnants of the brigade reached Kandahar. Out of a total of 2,476 of all ranks, engaged on this disastrous day, 964, including 20 officers, were killed, and 167, including 9 officers, wounded; 331 regimental followers and 201 horses were also killed, and 7 followers and 68 horses wounded.

From The Afghan Campaigns of 1878-1882 by Sidney H. Shad- bolt (Sampson Low, Marston, Searle and Rivington, 1882)

Chapter 4

The South Wales Borderers at Isandhlwana

The Zulu War of 1879 produced two tremendous shocks for the British public: one was the disaster at Isandhlwana, the other was the death of Prince Louis Napoleon, then serving with the British army.

The war had originated in a frontier dispute between Boers and Zulus but was in any case inevitable as a result of Cetewayo's ultra-militaristic policies; he would not allow his warriors to marry until they had done their quota of fighting, and the whole of Zululand was organized for fighting. As often happened, the British underestimated their opponents in the early stages and paid dearly for it. At Isandhlwana the 24th Foot (the South Wales Borderers), aided by some local levies, were wiped out by some fifteen thousand Zulus. They fought literally to the last round and the last man. It was this sort of performance which made British arms so respected throughout the world in the period of the British Empire; a British regiment might be outmanoeuvred, outnumbered and overwhelmed but its conquerors paid a price they could rarely afford. And eventually belated British reinforcements would arrive and the campaign would be won - unless the politicians decided to abandon the enterprise.

Henry Hallam Parr, who wrote this account, was a mile away at the time of the battle on reconnaissance, but came to the camp after the battle and also obtained first-hand accounts from Zulus later in the campaign.

(The South Wales Borderers have now joined with the Welch Regiment to form the Royal Regiment of Wales.)

And what had happened at Isandhlwana camp since we left it that morning?

When the force to attack Matyan moved out of camp on the morning of the 22nd, the Zulu army, some twenty thousand strong, under command of Umnyamana, was lying still in its bivouac in the valley of the 'Nguto range.

The force here collected consisted of the elite of the Zulu army, and included the king's bodyguard, the Undi corps, numbering nearly ten thousand men. The Tulwana, the king's special regiment, and the Nkobamakosi (or "the ringbenders ") were the two crack regiments of the Undi corps. These two were so jealous of each other that they had to be separated as much as possible to prevent fights occurring. It was not long ago that a serious fracas, resulting in many deaths, had taken place between the two regiments, on account of each regiment claiming the right to march first out of the king's kraal.

There were also the Nokenke, or "the dividers", and the Umhlanga, or "the rushes" — young regiments drafted on to an old corps of Chaka's, which had all but disappeared, being represented only by a few old men of seventy-eight or eighty years of age.

Then the Umcityu corps, "the sharp-pointed ones" - so called because in a quarrel which took place between Cetewayo and one of his brothers, part of the corps took one side and part another, which caused it to be compared to a stick pointed at both ends; the Uve and the Umbonambi, "the evil-seers", and the Nodwengu corps, who all considered themselves among the best of the Zulu army. The army then was lying still. No fires were allowed, lest they should betray to the white army the Zulu position.

No orders for an attack had been given, nor was it intended that an attack should be made that day, as it was new moon — in Zulu parlance, "the moon was dead", and it was an unlucky day. The attack was intended to take place the next day, the 23rd of January.

However, a part of the Umcityu corps, while changing its position from some reason or another, was seen and fired on by the scouts of No. 3 Column. The Zulus returned the fire, and other Zulu regiments then rose and ran to the sound of the firing, in no order or organization.

Discipline, however, was soon restored, and about 10 a.m. an organized attack on the position, according to Zulu tactics, was commenced. The Zulu front was, however, not parallel to ours, but the attack of their main body was directed on our left front.

The whole army moved round to the left front of the English position, sending out two horns, or flank attacks. These horns, continually lengthening, are supplied with men from the rear of the main body or chest of the army, which keeps up a steady and slow advance, until one or both of the horns have made good their ground, when the chest charges to overwhelm the enemy.

Even now, if the waggons, already inspanned, had been hastily laagered, merely drawn together, the oxen sent adrift, and the infantry collected inside with ammunition boxes, we should have been taught a sharp lesson, and should have had to deplore heavy loss, but not so terrible a disaster as that the tidings of which soon rang through South Africa and through the civilized world.

But about noon the die was cast, and two companies, under Captain Mostyn and Lieutenant Cavaye, were sent out to reinforce Shepstone's mounted natives on the left. Almost as soon, however, as the companies had come into action, it was found necessary for them to retire on the camp, because of the masses of the enemy which showed on their front and right front.

The position shortly after twelve o'clock was then as follows: -

To the front of the position, Durnford's mounted natives were retiring slowly on the camp before the Nkobamakosi and Umbonambi regiments, which must have numbered together nearly six thousand men, the Basutos taking advantage of every donga and defensible bit of ground to make a stand.

On the left, Shepstone's Basutos, supported by two companies 24th, were engaging a force of about eight thousand Zulus, composed of the Umcityu and Nokenke corps, and were retiring slowly before them on the camp; the fleet Zulus rapidly gaining on our men by rushing forward directly the fire slackened for a moment, which it necessarily did when the men turned about to retire.

By 12.30 Dumford's Basutos had reached, and were holding firmly, the donga which was at the foot of the camp. There were near and in the donga, as well as the Basutos, the Natal volunteers and police, and two companies of the 24th, and the tremendous fire kept up by this force entirely checked the Zulu attack on our front.

It must be remembered that the Zulus were attacking from our left front, so that the Zulu centre was opposed to our left and left centre.

On the left of the troops fighting near and in the donga, and in rear nearer the camp, were two other companies of the 24th, fronting towards the left front of the camp - one in extended order, and one (Younghusband's) seemingly held in reserve. Near the first of these companies the guns were in action. The two companies on the left in support of Shepstone's Basutos had now reached to within about two hundred and fifty or three hundred yards of the camp, and had got into a tolerably close formation, but were very short of ammunition.

At this time the Zulu regiments in front, who were suffering so heavily from the fire of the troops in the donga, showed signs of wavering, and all seemed going well for the defenders of the camp. The men were as cheery as possible, those belonging to the two companies on the left retiring coolly, and quite convinced in their own minds that they had come back for more ammunition, and would turn the tables on the Umcityu when they had refilled their pouches and could fire more rapidly; for the ammunition of these two companies had been rapidly expended, owing to the hot fire they had been forced to sustain, to keep the Zulus from closing upon them while they were retreating on the camp.

But while the attention of the English soldiers had been taken up in fighting the centre and left of the Zulu army, the right horn of the Zulus was rapidly getting into a position from which to clutch its enemy in the rear.

Behind the range of hills on the left of the position the right horn, unseen and unthought of, was warily and rapidly advancing. First, an officer, distinguished by his head ornament of leopard-skin, leading; then two or three warriors; then a cluster; then a continuous chain of men, thickening gradually as it stretched round toward the centre of the Zulu forces; - in this formation the Nodwengu corps, about four thousand strong, the men running and bounding in the air, encouraging one another with vehement gestures, silently made its way to the rear of the inaccessible hill, to take the doomed camp of the white men in reverse.

Just when the fire in the donga had begun slightly to slacken, and ammunition was being hurried out to all the companies, the leading warriors of the Nodwengu corps made their reappearance round the inaccessible hill in the rear of the camp. This sudden appearance of the first few men who were leading the Zulu right must have sent a thrill of dismay through every white man who saw the enemy had got into their rear.

The moment the Zulu regiments in front caught sight of the point of their right horn, they steadied and recommenced their attack.

Their advance was most rapid and determined. Skirmishing in long lines ten or twelve deep, with men in closer formation a short distance behind, they closed on the camp regardless of their losses. When the guns fired, those Zulus towards whom the guns were laid would fall flat, let the shell pass over them, then spring up with a shout of "Amoya!" ("It is only wind"), and again rush onwards.

At this time the two companies of the 24th were on the edge of the left of the camp, still holding the Umcityu regiment in check; but on the right the Umbonambi regiment, having separated itself from the Nkobamakosi and Uve, who were directly in front of the donga, made a determined rush into the camp on the right, and, keeping to their own right, took the troops who had been in the donga, and who were endeavouring to retire for ammunition to the waggons, in flank. At the same time the Umcityu charged the two companies on the left, and the Nodwengu poured in from the rear. The ranks of our men were thrown into more disorder by the men of the Native Contingent rushing away to endeavour to escape from their dreaded enemy, and the whole camp became one thick mass of Zulus surging in overwhelming numbers round the white men, fighting by companies, groups, or even singly.

The mounted Basutos, having managed to get their docile and hardy ponies out of the donga, fired two or three rounds at a point where the Zulus seemed weakest, and then charged, and many of them managed to escape.

The 24th, police, and volunteers were all endeavouring to close together, and to fight their way to the waggons for ammunition.

Younghusband's company, which has already been spoken of as having been held somewhat in reserve, was seemingly in square, and, with pouches tolerably full, was retiring steadily higher up the hill, drawing to it any stragglers who could reach it, and having the bandsmen of the regiment and the colours of the 2-2 4th in its centre.

The guns had been limbered up shortly before the charge of the Zulus, and had endeavoured to make their way from the left to the right of the camp; then, finding the road to Rorke's Drift barred, tried to discover a way of escape down the rocky valley leading to the Buffalo. But it was too late. As the guns charged through the Zulus, the gunners were assegaied on the limbers and the drivers on the horses. One gun was upset, Major Smith, who was killed near the bank of the Buffalo half an hour afterwards, being wounded in a gallant but ineffectual attempt to spike it; the horses of the other, maddened with pain and terror, galloped away towards a deep ravine about half a mile from the camp, and were found there afterwards, hanging stiff and stark in their harness over the precipice.

Of the desperate hand-to-hand combat now fought out to the last by the old and tried soldiers of the 24th and the brave little band of colonial troops, against overwhelming numbers, we shall never know the exact details. We can only form an idea of what occurred from those who caught a hurried glimpse of the scene while making their escape, and from the accounts of the Zulus themselves, weighing both by the sad evidence afforded by the position of our dead.

When the Umcityu and Nokenke regiments charged the two companies commanded by Mostyn and Cavaye, as they had just reached the camp the ranks turned back to back, and they fought sternly out to the end with the bayonet, without attempting to retire further.

"The red soldiers who had been out on the left," said an officer of the Umcityu, "they killed many of us with their bayonets. When they found we were upon them, they turned back to back. They all fought till they died. They were hard to kill; not one tried to escape."

One company, it is not clear which, seemed to have determined to cut its road through to Rorke's Drift, and by dint of desperate efforts and losing many men on its way, got on to and past the neck; but, weakened by its losses, it could get no further, and here a heap of gallant dead marked where its last stand was made.

While this company was fighting its way to the neck, Young- husband's taking up a position under Isandhlwana Hill, and Mostyn and Cavaye's being overwhelmed by the Umcityu, the two remaining companies under Wardell were, with the Natal police and volunteers, struggling together against the masses of the enemy, almost in the centre of the camp.

The Zulus, with keen and ready appreciation of gallantry, tell many tales of the way our men struggled on, fighting to the last, and how hard they struck before they could be subdued.
One tall man, a corporal of the 24th, killed four Zulus with his bayonet, but his weapon stuck for an instant in the throat of his last opponent, and the Zulus rushed in on him.

The only sailor in the camp, one of the men of Her Majesty's ship Active, was seen, his back against a waggon wheel, keeping the Zulus at bay with his cutlass; but a Zulu crept behind him, and stabbed him through the spokes.

One of the Natal volunteers, who had been sick in hospital, was found with his back against a stone near the hospital tent, nearly a hundred fired cartridges round him, his revolver empty, and his bowie-knife clutched in his hand.

Another quarter of an hour, at about half past one, and the scene has again changed. Except on the slopes close below the inaccessible hill, every white man is down among heaps of the enemy. The Zulus who have not begun to pillage have their attention turned to one point.

Below the inaccessible hill, as high up on its slopes as possible, is collected the remnant of the 24th. The company already mentioned as fighting in company square, having drawn to it a few stragglers and one or two officers who until now have escaped the assegai, has chosen the ground on which it means to die. It must have been quite clear to them that there was for them no chance of escape. There was only one point from which help could come, and the country could be seen for miles in that direction. Ammunition must have been then running low, and it was impossible for a fresh supply to be obtained, while the Zulu regiments were in swarms and in thousands round the hill. The Zulus (for no white man saw the end) tell the story - how firm the red soldiers stood; they describe the officers calling out and encouraging their men; they tell how often they charged the little square, till they became, after their heavy losses throughout the day, somewhat reluctant to attack it; they tell how the red soldiers even taunted them by gestures to come on; and then how at last, the white man's ammunition running short, they flung showers of assegais, standing just out of reach of the bayonet, and then rushed in and finished the one-sided fight.

"Ah, those red soldiers at Isandhlwana" many Zulus have said; "how few they were, and how they fought! They fell like stones, each man in his place."

From A Sketch of the Kaffir and Zulu Wars by Henry Hallam Parr (London, 1880)

Chapter 5

The Battle of Abu Klea

In January 1885 a huge Dervish army was besieging Khartoum where General Charles Gordon was Governor. The Dervishes were the fanatically brave followers of the Mahdi, a religious and military leader of exceptional quality. The strength of the Dervishes had not yet been appreciated by the British and Egyptians, nor did anyone seem to realize the difficulty of campaigning in the Sudan - yet.

The overland relief column, which consisted of men selected from a variety of regiments, was nearly wiped out at Abu Klea. At this time in this sort of terrain units would form themselves into a square to receive an expected attack. In the middle the stores and sick or wounded were placed. It was unthinkable that anyone could break into a British square but the Dervishes did in fact once accomplish it, though not at Abu Klea. Abu Klea was a murderous battle in which heat and thirst added to other problems. One of the casualties here was the redoubtable Colonel Fred Burnaby, believed by many to be the bravest man in the world.

The British Cabinet sent Colonel Charles Gordon to Khartoum, January 1884, to endeavour to evacuate the garrisons then in the Sudan, and as he could not do so, an expedition, under command of General Lord Wolseley, was ordered to relieve Gordon, Wolseley arriving at Cairo September 9th, 1884.

Practically the choice of routes was narrowed down to two. Disembarking on the shore of the Red Sea at Suakin, the expedition might strike across the desert to the Nile at Berber; or, concentrating in Lower Egypt, it might ascend the Nile. Each line of advance had its advocates, but Lord Wolseley decided in favour of the Nile route.

It does not fall within the limited scope of this description to detail all the manifold obstacles and incidents of the advance up the Nile in the 800 whale-boats sent out from England - how stores had to be amassed, camels collected, and other necessary preparations made. Suffice to say that, by the end of November, when the head of the long flotilla had reached Hannek, Lord Wolseley issued a stirring appeal "To the Sailors, Soldiers and Marines of the Nile Expedition", in which he dilated on the "glorious mission which the Queen had entrusted to them", and concluded: "We can - and with God's help will - save General Gordon from such a death."

To stimulate the energies of his men, Lord Wolseley offered a prize of £100 to the battalion which should make the quickest passage in its whale-boats up to Korti, a prize won by the Royal Irish, the Gordon Highlanders coming in second, and the West Kent men third.

A camp was formed at Korti, where Lord Wolseley established his headquarters, and by the middle of December the bulk of the expeditionary force was gathered there, with great part of its war material and stores.

Lord Wolseley divided his force into two separate columns - one commanded by Major-General Earle, and the other by Brigadier-General Sir Herbert Stewart. The former force, called the River Column, which numbered about 2,200 men, including the Black Watch and Gordon Highlanders, with six screw-guns, was to proceed up the Nile to punish the Monassir tribe for the murder of Colonel Stewart, who had accompanied Gordon to Khartoum, and who, on his way down the river again to Dongola, had been treacherously massacred, together with the gallant Mr. Frank Power, correspondent to The Times. After punishing the Monassirs, General Earle was to push on to Berber, thence to co-operate with Stewart in the relief of Khartoum.

Stewart was to march straight across the Bayuda desert to Metamneh. A glance at the map will show that, between Korti and Khartoum, the Nile makes a great sweep to the eastward, roughly like a bow well bent; and it was by the land-string of this bow that Stewart was directed to advance. Most of the column was mounted on camels.

The force at Stewart's disposal consisted of bluejackets, under Lord Charles Beresford; one squadron 19th Hussars (on horses); the Guards Camel Regiment, composed of selected men from the Guards and from the Royal Marines, under Colonel Boscawen; the Heavy Camel Regiment (Colonel Talbot), composed of selected men from the three Household and seven other cavalry regiments - Royals, Scots Greys, Bays, 4th and 5th Dragoon Guards, 5th and 16th Lancers; the Mounted Infantry Camel Regiment (Major Gough), composed of selected men from various regiments, most of whom had served in South Africa or Egypt; a detachment of Royal Engineers (Captain Dorward); half a battery Royal Artillery (Captain Norton); 400 men of the Royal Sussex (Major Sunderland); one company of the Essex Regiment; a bearer company; a movable field-hospital, and transport details. There was also a Light Camel Regiment, under Colonel Stanley Clarke, composed of selected men from nine cavalry regiments. A total of 2,000 combatants!

Various communications from Gordon had reached Lord Wolseley. On November 14th a message, which had been ten days on the road, to the effect that Khartoum could hold out for another forty days, but that "after that it would be difficult" - which meant that the relieving British force ought to be at Khartoum by about December 14th. But on the last day of the year, the day after a detachment of the Desert Column had made its first march, a second messenger reached headquarters at Korti and produced a tiny bit of paper, no larger than a postage stamp, which had been rolled up to the size of a pin and concealed in the seam of the man's garment. On this paper were the words: "Khartoum. All right. C.G.Gordon. 14 Dec., 1884."

But this sanguine-looking statement did not tally with the verbal information which the messenger had also been ordered to give to Lord Wolseley, and of which the general effect was expressed in one sentence: "We want you to come quickly." On the very day this messenger left Khartoum Gordon had written to a friend in Cairo: "All's up! I expect a catastrophe in ten days' time."

Sir Herbert Stewart, starting with the Camel Corps on December 30th, had occupied the wells of Gakdul, and leaving the Guards and stores returned to Korti.

On the morning of the 12th the column, struggling along, again reached the wells of Gakdul, which lie in a rocky, craterlike amphitheatre of the desert.

Early on the morning of the 14th the column, leaving a detachment of the Sussex Regiment to hold the wells, left Gakdul for the Nile. The column halted on a stony plateau January 16th, and bivouacked inside a zareba composed of stones, brushwood, baggage, and boxes.

The column stood to arms in the early morning of the 17th, and waited till dawn, when the fire from the hills became hot, and some Guards and Mounted Infantry were sent out to keep it down. While the column was waiting an attack, some Arab horsemen came round by the right but were soon dispersed by a few rounds of shell; and General Stewart determined to march out, leaving a small force behind to hold the zareba.

A square was formed and, about 9 a.m., marched down the valley towards a row of banners, while Barrow's Hussars moved off to the left to keep the enemy on the hills in check. The strength of the column - diminished as it was by the detachments which it had left behind to hold the zareba and the various wells in the rear - was now about 1,500 officers and men all told, with three screw-guns and one Gardner gun.

In the centre of the square were the camels, carrying water, ammunition, and hospital requirements. The rest of the camels, together with the sick and baggage, had been left in the zareba. On the square moving out of the hollow in which it had formed, it at once drew a brisk fire from the enemy's skirmishers, and already the men began to drop.

The square halted repeatedly to return the Arab fire and avoid having its rear face forced out by the sluggish camels.

When the square reached a point about five hundred yards from the Dervish banners it was again halted for the purpose of being "dressed", especially the rear face, which had again been bulged out by the lagging camels; but before the process could be completed, a mass of about 5,000 of the enemy suddenly started up from behind the flags, advanced at a quick run, in a serrated line, headed by horsemen, and charged down towards the left front corner of the square.

"When the enemy commenced the advance," wrote an officer, "I remember experiencing a feeling of pity mixed with admiration for them, as I thought they would all be shot down in a few minutes ... As they advanced, the feeling was changed to wonder that the tremendous fire we were keeping up had so little effect. When they got within eighty yards, the fire of the Guards and Mounted Infantry began to take good effect, and a huge pile of dead rose in front of them. Then, to my astonishment, the enemy took ground to their right rapidly, but in order, as if on parade, so as to envelop the rear of the square. I remember thinking, 'By Jove, they will be into the square!' and almost the next moment I saw a fine old sheikh on horseback plant his banner in the centre of the square, behind the camels. He was at once shot down, falling on his banner.

"Directly the sheikh fell, the Arabs began running in under the camels to the front part of the square. Some of the rear rank now faced about and began firing. By this time Herbert Stewart's horse was shot, and as he fell three Arabs ran at him. I was close to his horse's tail, and disposed of the one nearest to me, about three paces off, and the others were, I think, killed by the Mounted Infantry officers close by . . . There was one strange incident. An unwounded Arab, armed with a spear, jumped up and charged an officer. The officer grasped the spear with his left hand, and with his right ran through the Arab's body, and there for a few seconds they stood, the officer being unable to withdraw his sword until a man ran up and shot the Arab. It was a living embodiment of the old gladiatorial frescoes at Pompeii.

"I was much struck with the demeanour of the Guards officers. There was no noise or fuss; all the orders were given as if on parade, and they spoke to the men in a quiet manner, as if nothing unusual was going on."

Colonel Burnaby, of Khiva fame, went outside the square. An eyewitness - Mr. Bennett Burleigh, of The Daily Telegraph - thus described the scene that followed:

"As the dauntless Colonel rode forward on a borrowed nag - for his own had been shot that morning - he put himself in the way of a sheikh charging down on horseback. Ere the Arab closed with him a bullet from someone in our ranks, and not Burnaby's sword-thrust, brought the sheikh to the ground. The enemy's spearmen were close behind, and one of them suddenly dashed at the Colonel, pointing the long blade of his spear at his throat. Checking his horse and slowly pulling it backward, Burnaby leaned forward in his saddle and parried the Moslem's rapid thrusts; but the length of the man's weapon - eight feet - put it out of his power to return with interest the Arab's murderous intent. Once or twice, I think, the Colonel just touched his man, only to make him more wary and eager. The affray was the work of three or four seconds only, for the savage horde of swarthy negroes from Kordofan, and the straight-haired tawny complexioned Arabs of the Bayuda steppes, were fast closing in upon our square. Burnaby fenced smartly, just as if he were playing in an assault-at-arms, and there was a smile on his features as he drove off the man's awkward thrusts.
"The scene was taken in at a glance - with that lightning instinct which I have seen the desert warriors before now display in battle while coming to one another's aid - by an Arab, who, pursuing a soldier, had passed five paces to Burnaby's right and rear. Turning with a sudden spring, this second Arab ran his spear-point into the colonel's right shoulder. It was but a slight wound — enough, though, to cause Burnaby to twist round in his saddle to defend himself from this unexpected attack. Before the savage could repeat his blow, a soldier ran out and drove his sword-bayonet through the second assailant. As the Englishman withdrew the steel, the ferocious Arab wriggled round and sought to reach him. The effort was too much, however, and the man reeled and fell.

"Brief as was Burnaby's glance backward at this fatal episode, it was long enough to enable the first Arab to deliver his spear- point full in the brave officer's throat. The blow drove Burnaby out of the saddle, but it required a second one before he let go his grip of the reins and tumbled upon the ground. Half a dozen Arabs were now about him. With the blood gushing in streams from his gashed throat, the dauntless Guardsman leaped to his feet, sword in hand, and slashed at the ferocious group. They were the wild strokes of a proud, brave man, dying hard. Private Wood, of the Grenadier Guards, sprang to his rescue, but it was too late, for the Colonel was overborne and fell to the ground. Wood raised his head, and, seeing that the case was hopeless, exclaimed: 'Oh, Colonel, I fear I can say no more than "God Bless you!" ' The dying man, his life-blood running out in a stream from his jugular vein, opened his eyes, smiled, gave a gentle pressure of the hand, and passed away."

Changing their original direction towards the left front of the square, the Arabs had come down on the left rear corner with lightning speed. They had been quick to "spot" the square's most vulnerable point, which was where it had been bulged out by the camels. The last hundred yards were crossed in a few seconds, although during this brief space numbers fell before the fire of the "Heavies" and the Gardner gun, which the Naval Brigade had run out about twenty yards outside the left rear face. But the number of rifles was insufficient to annihilate the masses of Arabs who came rushing on, and in a few seconds the left rear corner was pressed back by sheer weight of numbers. Unfortunately, too, the Gardner gun jammed, and caused the loss of nearly half the Naval Brigade, who gallantly stood by it until they were slaughtered or swept into the square by the rush of Arabs.

The jamming of the Gardner gun was thus described by Lord Charles Beresford, commanding the Naval Brigade: "The Gardner gun jammed after firing about thirty rounds. The enemy were then about two hundred yards from the muzzle of the gun. The captain of the gun, Will Rhoods, chief boatswain's mate, and myself, unscrewed the plate to clear the barrel or take the lock of the jammed barrel out, when the enemy were upon us. Rhoods was killed with a spear. Walter Miller, armourer, I also saw killed with a spear at the same moment on my left. I was knocked down in the rear of the gun, but uninjured, except a small spear-scratch on the left hand. The crowd and crush of the enemy was very great at this point, and, as I struggled up, I was carried against the face of the square, which was literally pressed by sheer weight of numbers about twelve paces from the position of the gun.

"The crush was so great that at the moment few on either side were killed, but fortunately this flank of the square had been forced up a very steep little mound, which enabled the rear rank to open a tremendous fire over the heads of the front rank men; this relieved the pressure, and enabled the front rank to bayonet or shoot those of the enemy nearest them. The enemy then, for some reason, turned to their right along the left flank of the square, and streamed away in numbers along the rear face of it. In a very few minutes the terrific fire from the square told on the enemy. There was a momentary waver, and then they walked quietly away. I immediately manned the Gardner, and cleared the jam as soon as I could. This, however, was not done in time to be of much use in firing on the slowly retreating enemy, as they had got back into the nullah and behind the mound before it was ready."

The onrush of the furious Arabs - brandishing their weapons and yelling out their "Allah-il-Allah!" - was compared with the rolling on of a vast wave of black surf. About 12,000 of them were estimated to have been on the ground, though only about of these took part in the actual attack - 5,000 against 1,500! It was no wonder that, at the first impact of this impetuous mass of raging devils, the British square - a formation which has become a synonym for impregnable stability - had been dented in and thrown into momentary confusion. Indeed, for some little time, the fate of this handful of England's finest fighting men trembled in the balance. "I think," wrote Lieutenant Douglas Dawson, "that all present would never care to see a nearer shave than this, and it is, in my opinion, due to the fact that the two sides not immediately attacked (the front and right) stood their ground that the enemy retired discomfited. Had the Guards moved, none of us would have lived to tell the tale."

At one time it looked as if the two remaining sides of the square must be "swallowed up by the hordes surrounding us; so much so that, seeing my brother a few paces off, I rushed to him, shook his hand hard, and returned to my place . . . Setting their feet apart for better purchase, our Guardsmen refused to budge one inch; we put our rear rank about, and they shot down or bayoneted every Arab that came near them."

By sheer weight of the Arab rush, the left face of the square was gradually forced back to close to the rear of the front face. The camels, which had hitherto been a source of weakness to the square, now became a source of strength; for, when the rear face was also forced in, the camels formed a living traverse that broke the Arab rush, and gave time for the right and front faces to take advantage of the higher ground on which they stood and fire over the heads of those engaged in a desperate hand to hand struggle on the surging masses of the enemy behind. The centre of the square became the scene of a most desperate conflict - camels, horses, men, all involved in one sanguinary welter.

Within the square the din of battle was such that no words of command could be heard, and each man was obliged to act on the impulse of the moment, and fight for his own hand.

The Arabs were only inside the square for some minutes, when the little band of 1,500 British soldiers "had by sheer pluck and muscles killed the last of the fanatics who had penetrated into their midst." At the same time, the fire of the "Heavies" and Royal Sussex had checked a formidable charge of Arab cavalry towards the right rear corner of the square. When the inside of the square was at last cleared, its outside assailants drew off.

The battle had been as bloody as it was brief - 1,100 dead Arab bodies were counted in the immediate neighbourhood of the square; their loss in wounded was exceptionally heavy.

But our victory had been as dearly, as it was narrowly, bought. The Arabs' spears and swords had done ghastly execution during that terrible five minutes of the fray. "I went out to help about the water, etc.", wrote Sir C. Wilson, "and found the spot where the square had been broken a horrible sight - too horrible for description." Nine officers were killed, and 65 non-commissioned officers and men; while the wounded (including Lord Airlie) numbered nine officers (two of whom afterwards died), and 85 non-commissioned officers and men.

From this scene of carnage the square was moved away a few hundred yards to pull itself together again; and then, while the wounded were being attended to, and the enemy's arms, ammunition, etc., burnt, the Hussars were sent forward to find the wells. The men were suffering agonies of thirst, but said nothing. At last the column reached the Abu-Klea wells, of which the muddy water tasted to all like champagne after the exertions of the day. Here the force bivouacked for a cold and miserable night without stores and baggage.

Next morning (18th) a small fort was built for the protection of the wounded, and left under a guard of 100 men of the Royal Sussex; and in the afternoon the column again moved off for Metamneh, about 23 miles distant, to strike the Nile - and for a sight of the Nile Stewart's thirst-afflicted men were now yearning.

All that day the column moved forward through bush; the head of the column came out on open ground about 1 a.m. (on the 19th), and then, after a short halt, it marched till dawn (about 6 a.m.), when the return of daylight revived the spirits of both men and animals. The column was about five miles west of the river, and the same distance south of Metamneh. To traverse the 18 miles from Abu-Klea had taken fourteen hours!

At 7.30 a.m., from a gravel ridge the Nile, with Shendy and Metamneh, appeared in sight. But a formidable force of Arabs stood between the column and the Nile, with intent to dispute its approach to the deeply-longed-for water.

A zareba was formed on open ground upon a small hill of gravel, commanding the surrounding expanse of grass and bush - about four miles from the Nile. The column breakfasted under fire. Mr. Cameron, the gallant war correspondent of the Standard and Mr. St. Leger Herbert, of the Morning Post, who was also acting as private secretary to Sir Herbert Stewart, were killed.

From British Battles on Land and Sea by Field Marshal Sir Evelyn Wood (Cassell, 1915)

Chapter 6

The Battle of Omdurman

Although the Mahdi had died in 1885 soon after the fall of Khartoum the Dervish empire continued under his successor, the Khalifa, and eventually extended over about a million square miles. Its rule became tyrannical and after ten years it became obvious to the British Government that if they did not send an expedition to restore order and justice one of their European rivals, the Germans or French perhaps, would do so instead.

The re-conquest was begun in 1896 and, owing to the vastness of the country and the difficulties of climate and terrain, took two years. The Commander in Chief (Sirdar) was Kitchener, a former Royal Engineer who was well-suited for the task though a poor field-commander (he had plenty of dashing subordinates who were capable of fighting battles). The Khalifa apparently believed that if he fought his enemies within sight of the Mahdi's tomb all would go well. Kitchener's forces therefore reached the plain of Omdurman, just outside Khartoum, without having met the full weight of the Dervish army, though not without having fought some battles. Omdurman, on 2 September 1898, was notable for the astonishing courage of the Dervishes, the steadiness of the British/Egyptian force, and the charge of the 21st Lancers in which Winston Churchill took part.

The date for the attack on Omdurman was determined by the fact that the Nile between Berber and Khartoum would be at its highest about the end of August and the beginning of September. The Sirdar's plan was to complete the concentration of his army in the first half of August, and begin the advance about the middle of the month. He would thus be able to make the fullest use of the Nile for transport by water of troops and supplies in the first stage of the advance, and for the operations of his gunboat flotilla in the actual fighting, although at this time the climate would be very trying for Europeans.

By the middle of August the Sirdar's army, about 22,000 strong, had concentrated along the Nile from the Atbara to Wad Hamed, near the Shabluka cataract, the transports being used to save the European infantry, and for carriage of stores.

There were two infantry divisions, the British, composed of two brigades, and the Egyptian of four.
British Division - General Gatacre
1st Brigade — Colonel A. Wauchope: 1st Cameron Highlanders; 1st Seaforth Highlanders; 1st Lincolnshire; 1st Royal Warwickshire.
2nd Brigade - Colonel the Hon. Neville Lyttelton: 1st Grenadier Guards; 1st Rifle Brigade; 1st Northumberland Fusiliers; 2nd Lancashire Fusiliers.
Egyptian Division - General Archibald Hunter
1st Brigade - Colonel Hector Macdonald: 2nd Egyptians;
9th, 10th, and 11h Sudanese.
2nd Brigade - Colonel Maxwell: 8th Egyptians; 12th, 13th, and 14th Sudanese.
3rd Brigade - Colonel Lewis: 3rd, 4th, 7th, and 15th Egyptians.
4th Brigade - Colonel Collinson: 1st, 5th, and 17th, and 18th Egyptians.

To the British Division there were attached a battery of six Maxims, manned by men of the 16th Company E.D., R.A.; a battery of four Maxims, manned by 1st Royal Irish Fusiliers; and a detachment of No. 2 Company R.E.

To the Egyptian Division were attached six Maxims, manned by Egyptian gunners. The mounted troops were: 21st Lancers, Colonel Martin; 10 squadrons of Egyptian cavalry, Colonel Broadwood; and eight companies of the Camel Corps (Egyptian Mounted Infantry), Major Tudway.

The Egyptian cavalry had with them Maxims mounted on galloping carriages, drawn by mules.

The artillery consisted of seven batteries and a detachment of the Light siege-train, 44 guns in all, organized as follows:

British Artillery - 32nd Battery, R.A., six 15-pounders; 37th Battery, R.A., six 5-inch howitzers, throwing a 50-pound shell; detachment 16th Company E.D., R.A., with two 40-pounder siege Krupp guns, throwing a 9½ pound shell; four field batteries of quick-firing guns, six to each battery.

The army was to advance on Omdurman by the west bank of the Nile. At the same time Captain Keppel's flotilla of 14 gun-boats was to steam up the river, and a force of 3,000 friendly Arabs, under Major Stuart-Wortley, Egyptian Army, was to march up the east bank.

August 31st. Colonel Broadwood, with the Egyptian cavalry and Camel Corps, the horse battery and three Maxims, sweeping away to the right, approached Omdurman on its western side. Meanwhile the 21st Lancers advanced direct on the city, between Broadwood's line of march and the Nile, passing through Kerreri, which had been evacuated by the Dervishes. Broadwood occupied the hill of Jebel Fereid, five miles west of the centre of the city.

Presently the war-drums began to beat in Omdurman, and from its seven miles of western front the Khalifa's warriors came, with hundreds of fluttering standards, to serve as rallying points. As they gained the open plain they formed in five great masses, and then advanced. Broadwood gave the order to retire. The Lancers had come up on the Dervish right, and as the enemy advanced they exchanged a few shots with them. But the Dervishes did not come on. Having watched for a while the retirement of the mounted troops, they went back into Khartoum.

Whilst this reconnaissance was in progress Captain Keppel had steamed up to the end of Tuti Island with four gunboats, and had carefully observed the river defences. On the way up he had shelled and set on fire a Dervish camp on the hills between Kerreri and Omdurman.

The Sirdar had his army in bivouac at a small ruined village about a mile and a half south of Kerreri. The camp was shaped like a capital D, the straight side of it being along the Nile bank, and the curved facing the desert. This line was fortified partly with a zareba hedge, partly with shelter trenches. Guns and Maxims were placed at intervals. Inside the camp a few houses afforded shelter for the field hospital.

The ground immediately in front of the camp was a slightly undulating plain about a mile wide, across which an attacking force must advance with very little cover from fire. Beyond the plain were some low hills, and to the left rose a bald, rocky mass, marked on the map as Jebel Surgham.

Early on the Thursday morning Keppel had taken six gunboats across the river to a point just below Halfiya.

Major Stuart-Wortley's army of friendlies marched along the eastern river bank, a motley crowd of many tribes, the Jaalin tribesmen leading. A number of mounted Dervish scouts retired towards Halfiya. Close to the village there were two forts on the river bank. These were bombarded by the gunboats, and in a few minutes what was left of the garrison took to flight. Meanwhile the scouts, who had pushed on in front, rode in with the news that the enemy were holding a group of four small villages near the river bank opposite Omdurman.

The gunboats sent a shower of shells into the villages. Then Stuart-Wortley moved up and got into the Dervish position. There was a short fight with spear and sword, and the enemy were driven out, losing some 300 men, including several of their Emirs.

The enemy having been disposed of, the howitzer battery and its escort were landed. Stuart-Wortley and the range-finders, with an escort of fifty of the friendlies, searched for a good position for the guns on the Nile bank. Major Stuart-Wortley and Lieutenant Buckle, R.A., were approaching the river bank with 10 dismounted friendlies, followed by Lieutenant Wood, Staff officer (a son of the first Sirdar*), when suddenly 30 Baggara horsemen who had rallied from the Dervish rout, and returned to the scene of the fight, came on at a wild gallop. So fierce and sudden was their onset that the friendlies bolted in confusion. While Wortley was getting the 10 dismounted friendlies on to their knees, the Baggara leader charged Lieutenant Wood and his Syrian interpreter. The Baggara's spear missed Wood's ear. Putting his revolver into the Baggara's face, he blew his head off. Then the friendlies rallied, and the remnant of the Baggaras galloped off at speed.

*Sir Evelyn Wood, VC.

A good position having been found on the east bank just north of the point of Tuti Island, the howitzers were placed in battery by Major Elmslie and opened fire on Omdurman, taking for their guiding mark the great white dome of the Mahdi's tomb. Keppel and the flotilla meanwhile engaged and rapidly destroyed a large fort on Tuti Island, and then crossed the Nile and steamed slowly along the river front of Omdurman, engaging the riverside forts in succession one by one, silencing and wrecking each with a shower of shells and Maximum bullets before going on to the next.

The howitzers meanwhile were sending their shells curving high in air over the gunboats and dropping them into the city beyond. One of them smashed in the side of the white dome on the Mahdi's tomb, and another wrecked the central building of his palace. Gaps wide enough to drive a carriage through were torn in the riverside wall, the masonry being fairly blasted away by the explosion.

Having silenced the Omdurman batteries, the flotilla steamed on to attack a fort on the point of land between the two Niles close to the ruins of Khartoum - the Mukran Fort of Gordon's diaries. After a short fight the garrison were driven out, and fled inland.

The Khalifa Abdullahi and his Emirs realised that to sit fast in the entrenched position of Omdurman was to run the risk of being killed in detail without having the chance of even striking a blow, and determined, therefore, to come and fight in the open.

The cavalry reported that the Dervish army was 30,000 strong. The Sirdar, who had ridden forward to Jebel Surgham at noon to have a look at the enemy, estimated them at 35,000, but he says in his report: " from subsequent information this figure was probably under-estimated, their actual strength being between and 50,000."

In quality as well as in mere numbers it was the most powerful and best-equipped force that had ever been gathered on one field in the Mahdist movement. There were about 10,000 riflemen, but the cartridges, manufactured in the Khalifa's workshops, were very defective, and loaded with bad powder; the riflemen never had any target practice, and mostly regarded the sights of their Remingtons as useless appendages; and their leaders had never heard of such a thing as infantry fire tactics. The fire of the Jehadia was only effective at close quarters.

The riflemen were supplemented by some 20,000 spear and swordsmen, 2,000 of whom were horsemen of the Baggara tribe. There was practically no artillery - three small Krupps, for which the ammunition was poor.

The Sirdar had timed his advance so as to arrive before Omdurman when the moon was near the full. Bright nights enabled some of the marching to be done in the cool moonlight, and it minimised the danger of attacks by the enemy.

The night before the battle was clear and bright, and to give additional security to the riverside camp, the gunboats, moored close to the Nile bank, swept its flanks and front with the broad white beams from their electric searchlights.

The position of the British army was a mile and a half long, its flanks thrown back so as to rest on the Nile, its shape a flattened curve. There was a mile along the river bank from tip to tip of this bent bow formed by the fighting line, the broadest point between the curve and the river being about a thousand yards. In the space thus enclosed were the mudwalled huts of the village of Agaiga, under the shelter of which the field hospital had been established. Near the river bank the transport animals were massed, some 3,000 camels and 1,000 mules.

The left of the line was formed by the British Division - Lyttelton's brigade nearest the Nile, then Wauchope's. The 32nd Battery of the Royal Artillery, two Egyptian field batteries, and the Maxim battery, manned by the Royal Irish Fusiliers, were in the part of the line held by Lyttelton. In the centre were Maxwell's and Lewis's brigades of the Egyptian army, and on the right, facing northwards, with its flank resting on a creek that ran into the Nile, was Macdonald's Sudanese brigade. In the intervals of that part of the line held by the Egyptian army there were two Egyptian batteries and some Maxims. The 4th Egyptian Brigade, under Collinson, was in reserve inside the line on the right. The front held by the British Division was covered by a zareba hedge of desert thorn bushes. The Egyptian brigades had no zareba, but had dug a shelter trench all along their position. The Camel Corps, Broadwood's Egyptian cavalry, and the Horse Artillery were on the extreme right, near the river, well outside the curved line of battle. The gunboat flotilla lay along the river front of the camp. On the east side of the Nile were Stuart-Wortley's friendlies and the howitzer battery in position near Halfiya. As soon as the sun was up the howitzers again began dropping shells into Omdurman.

By five o'clock the whole force was ready to march, but before breaking up the position and moving to the attack of the Dervishes the Sirdar waited for news from the cavalry. The word was passed that the enemy was advancing to the attack of the camp. It was a piece of good fortune for the Anglo-Egyptian army - with an open field of fire extending for nearly three thousand yards to the front, and with flanks resting on the river, and covered by the quick-firing guns of the flotilla. The Khalifa was throwing away every chance by attacking our troops while they were still in their position.

The Khalifa's first line was formed of five great masses of rifle and spearmen, on a front of between two and three miles. In the rear of it there was a second line, of much less strength, escorting a mass of camels and donkeys laden with supplies. Horsemen were riding on the flanks and here and there in the intervals of the great moving mass of infantry.

On the British left, Major William's R.F.A. 15-pounders opened at 6.40 a.m. on the Dervish right flank with shrapnel, at yards range, with good effect. Then the others joined in, and all along the Dervish front the bursting shells tore gaps in their ranks, gaps that were filled up, however, as soon as they were made.

Under the rain of bursting shells and Maxims and Lee-Metford bullets the Dervishes came on. The quick-firing guns of the flotilla were brought to bear on them, but there was no check in their advance; and now the infantry added the bullets of some thousands of rifles to the storm of fire that was pouring from all the curving front of the camp. Some of the Dervishes replied, and the front of their advance was white with drifting smoke. They had got their Krupp guns into action on the shoulder of Jebel Surgham, but the shells burst some hundreds of yards short of the British Division. At this stage of the attack the losses of the Dervishes must have been enormous, but still they advanced, their front line, torn by bullet and shell, being within 800 yards of the camp.

The left attack, directed by the Khalifa's son Osman, poured over the slopes of the Kerreri Hills, its objective being the right of the Sirdar's line. But it came in contact with the mass of the mounted troops, which, to avoid being crushed by the mere weight of superior numbers, were retiring northwards along the Nile. At first Broadwood moved his squadrons slowly, bringing Major Young's horse battery into action against the Dervishes and harassing them with the carbine fire of his dismounted troopers to cover the retirement of Tudway's Camel Corps. But his small force was so hard pressed by the thousands of Dervishes, firing heavily as they came, that he had at last to leave the Camel Corps, which were in imminent danger of being destroyed, to be effectually covered by the devastating fire of two gunboats on the river bank, which absolutely crushed the Dervish attack. Screened by the spur of the hills that runs towards the river near Kerreri from any fire from the camp, the Dervish column had pushed in between the mounted troops and the Sirdar's infantry.

They poured such a heavy rifle fire into the battery that numbers of the horses were killed or maimed, and it was impossible to fully horse more than four of the guns. The other two were temporarily abandoned, the gunners carrying off with them the breech blocks. The Camel Corps, marching along the Nile bank under cover of the flotilla guns, rode into the north end of the camp and formed up behind the right flank of Macdonald's brigade.

While this was happening, Colonel Broadwood, with the cavalry and the four guns of the horse battery, had retreated to the northward, the cavalry acting sometimes with carbine fire dismounted, sometimes charging the Dervish horse when it ventured to press closely on the battery in action. When the pressure on his force lessened, he turned, and, marching along the Nile, worked his way back towards the main battle-field. Broadwood's fight had a useful result on the fortunes of the day; for a moment it had diverted at least 10,000 of the Khalifa's troops from the attack on the main position.

Let us now turn to what was being done on the main battlefield. When the Dervish right and centre attacks had advanced to about 800 yards, the British brigades standing behind zarebas suffered slight loss. The Sudanese and Egyptian regiments were much better off in their shelter trenches. Shallow as they were, they afforded good cover to a kneeling line, and very complete protection to men lying down, and both positions mean a steadier aim for the firing line.

For five minutes the Dervish fire was heavy. There was said to have been at least ten thousand riflemen engaged in this first onslaught upon the camp. For the success of the Dervish horsemen and spearmen there was no hope but in getting to close quarters with the defenders of the camp, and they pressed on recklessly, wave upon wave, mostly to fall as they came up within 500 yards' range, or to limp back disabled. But the riflemen found some little shelter here and there behind the undulations of the desert ground, and lying down they kept up a fire in comparative security. Some of them established themselves within 400 yards of the British zareba hedge, and at that range their Remingtons did some damage.

The guns on the left and the Maxims had been run out till they formed almost a right angle with the south side of the zareba, so as to enfilade the enemy's attack. For half an hour, through the hail of bullet and shell, the Dervishes came on. The Khalifa's Black Standard, a flag about six feet square, flying from a long bamboo lance ornamented with silver, was in front of the array that bore down upon Maxwell's brigade. Naturally the Black Standard attracted a heavy fire, and through the field-glasses man after man was seen to fall while carrying it. But it was hardly down when it was flying again in the hands of another warrior.

So rapid was the fire from the British front that the rifles became too hot to hold. They were carried by the leather slings back to the companies waiting in reserve behind the firing line, who handed their weapons to their comrades standing at the zareba hedge. Occasionally reserve men were themselves called up to fire, while the men who had already been in action rested and refilled their cartridge pouches. By half-past seven the dash of the Dervish onset began to visibly diminish. Hundreds of their bravest had fallen. They were beginning to realise that it was impossible to get closer than five to six hundred yards from the Anglo-Egyptian front. There for a full mile along the desert lay the dead and dying, piled up in heaps or stretched in ghastly rows.

A last effort was made by them in the centre against the Egyptian front, even after the Mahdists had given up the attack on the British and were falling back along the death-strewn slopes of Jebel Surgham. This attack, too, gradually flickered and went out in a patter of musketry. Towards eight o'clock the rifle fire from the Sirdar's line had all but ceased. The batteries' guns were still in action and the gunboats shelled the hills over which the Dervishes were hurriedly retreating.

By half-past eight it looked as if the battle was over. The enemy had withdrawn over the slopes of the Kerreri Hills on one side and of Jebel Surgham on the other. The Sirdar had determined to push on at once for Omdurman, about five miles distant, so as to reach it before the Dervishes could rally for its defence. This was a tactical error, for the Khalifa still had over undefeated men west of Jebel Surgham.

The force was ordered to advance in direct echelon of brigades from the left, which moved on the Nile bank. Each brigade was in a line of columns at deploying intervals. Distance was lost, firstly, because the European Division moved southwards while General Hunter's infantry moved westwards to get into echelon; and, secondly, because that experienced officer held back his most reliable brigade and his most experienced Brigadier, Hector Macdonald, to move on the outer, i.e. exposed flank of the echelon.

Along the river bank and farther back came the Camel Corps and the Egyptian cavalry. Collinson's brigade formed up to escort the transport train along the Nile bank, and serve as a reserve to the whole.

The Sirdar sent orders to Colonel Martin to take the 21st Lancers out in front of the British Division, over the long slope that ran down from Jebel Surgham to the river, and find out if any portion of the Dervishes had rallied behind it on the line of advance, and drive them across the British front into the desert, but he ordered the infantry to advance without awaiting the result, practically simultaneously.

Passing round to the south-east of Jebel Surgham, Colonel Martin saw scattered Dervishes retiring landwards. About half a mile south of the ridge, the ground scouts reported that about 200 of the enemy were hiding in a hollow that ran down to the river. Beyond the hollow could be seen some thirty Dervish horsemen. The impression conveyed by this report, and by what could be seen from the ground the regiment occupied, was that a small party of the enemy who had taken part in the attack on the camp were waiting for a chance to escape.

Colonel Martin decided to get between the enemy and their line of retreat landwards, so the Lancers moved to the westward of the hollow and formed up for the charge.

When the regiment was 300 yards from the enemy the men could see that the scouts had made a mistake, and that there was no mere handful of beaten Dervishes in their front, but a dense crowd of rifle and spearmen, packed together in the rocky khor. Colonel Martin, in front of the centre squadron, rode straight for where the broad Sudan spears bristled most thickly.

A minute more and the Lancers were into the mass of Dervish infantry, dashing through a storm of bullets and leaping down a drop into the hollow, where the enemy stood twenty deep. In about one minute 320 troopers had ridden over and through at least 1,500 foemen. But into those brief moments there were crowded many deeds of devoted heroism.

The centre squadron, striking the Dervish line where the crowd was thickest, suffered most. Several of the horses struck by the bullets had held on till the check came as they struck the Dervish line.

Then they fell, and it fared badly with their riders. Other horses were brought down by spear thrusts and hamstringing cuts with sword and knife; for the enemy showed no fear of the horsemen, and stood up pluckily. Lieutenant the Hon. R. F. Molyneux, Royal Horse Guards, attached to the Lancers, lost his horse just before reaching the hollow, the animal, riddled by a bullet, dropping dead. The lieutenant ran on into the crowd on foot, revolver in hand. Two Dervishes attacked him. He shot one, but as he did so the other brought down his long sword on the officer's right arm, gashing it badly and making him drop his pistol. He thus found himself unarmed in the midst of the enemy. He ran, pursued by the swordsmen, and got up the farther slope just as the Lancers rallied, and faced the Dervishes again, after riding through them. A corporal came out from the ranks, gave Molyneux his stirrup leather, and brought him safely out of the struggle. Surgeon-Major Pinches, whose horse had been shot under him, was saved by Sergeant-Major Brennan, who, after cutting down several of his assailants, got the Major behind him on his horse and rode out of the khor. Lieutenant Robert Grenfell, who was leading a troop of the centre squadron, was thrown by his wounded horse, but made a desperate fight on foot. He fired every shot in his revolver, and when last seen alive was facing several spearmen, sword in hand.

In less than two minutes the Lancers had more than 70 casualties. Of the horses, 119 were killed, many of them just struggling out of the hollow and falling dead as the regiment rallied close to the enemy. It was during this rally that some of the bravest deeds were done, individual officers riding back to bring off wounded or dismounted comrades. Major Wyndham had lost his horse, and was trying to mount behind Lieutenant Smyth, who had turned back to help him. He had failed in two attempts, when he was lifted up by Captain Kenna, who came riding back, accompanied by Lieutenant de Montmorency and Corporal Swarbrick, all bent on saving young Grenfell, if he still lived, and, if not, carrying off his body. Grenfell was lying on the nearer slope of the hollow, and a number of Dervishes were hacking at him with their swords. Kenna and his comrades drove them off with their pistols, and while the corporal held two of the horses, the two officers tried to lift Grenfell's body on to the third. The Lieutenant was quite dead, bleeding from more than a dozen wounds. As they placed the body across the saddle the horse shied and bolted, throwing it to the ground. The three would-be rescuers had then to retire, keeping off the pursuing Dervishes with their revolvers.

Hardly a man or horse escaped without some injury, and in every troop horses and men were bleeding from wounds, some slight, but in many cases serious, for all were trying to keep their places in the ranks, afraid only of being ordered to fall out. Lieutenant Brinton, of the Life Guards, with his left shoulder cut open, took his place at the head of his troop as if he were un-wounded.

Officers and men were eager to charge back through the enemy but Colonel Martin decided that enough had been done. He dismounted a number of troopers and opened fire with carbines on the

Dervishes, who, after firing a few shots in reply, retreated towards the hills from the hollow which no longer protected them. As they did so they were forced to cross the front of the British Division. The guns of the 32nd Battery unlimbered and poured shrapnel into them. The infantry gave them volley after volley, and only a small number of them reached the shelter of the hills.

Sixty dead Dervishes were found in the hollow; a number of wounded men got away from it when they retired. Several hundred were killed as they retreated across the plain.

While the Lancers were charging the Dervishes on the other side of the Jebel Surgham ridge, the infantry brigades, British and Egyptian, were moving out from the ground they had held in the echelon formation. The leading British brigade, Lyttelton's, marching due south, was just topping the sandy ridge between Surgham and the river, and Wauchope's brigade had drawn up nearly level with it. The Sirdar and his Staff were riding close to them when the approach of some riderless horses at 9.30 a.m. indicated the 21st Lancers' charge.

The brigades of Generals Maxwell and Lewis were somewhat in rear, marching south-west towards Jebel Surgham; General Collinson's brigade and the transport were moving southwards on the Nile bank. The field hospitals were being packed, but 150 wounded were still on the ground, the only troops at hand being a few Europeans and three companies of an Egyptian battalion. There was a gap of nearly half a mile between Lewis's right and Macdonald's left; the latter having 18 guns and eight Maxims. At this time, screened by the hills that looked down on the morning's battle-field, the Khalifa was gathering his army for another great effort. The warriors engaged in this second attack had, for the most part, taken no share in the earlier one. The Dervishes were massed in two huge columns, which were to make a converging attack on the Egyptian right and right rear. The left column, composed largely of those who had been in action against Colonel Broadwood and the mounted troops, was commanded by the Khalifa's son Osman and the Emir Ali Wad Helu. The right column was commanded by Yakub, the Khalifa's brother, and the Khalifa himself accompanied it. Macdonald's brigade, about 3,000 infantry, was accompanied by three of the Egyptian batteries of quick-firers. These were commanded respectively by Majors Peak, Lawrie, and Captain de Rougemont. Macdonald had also with him eight Maxim guns. It was fortunate that he was so strong in artillery, for on his isolated brigade the storm of the Dervish attack burst in its full fury.

He had a brief warning from an advance of the Dervish cavalry of what was coming. Then, as he deployed his brigade in line facing south-west, Yakub's column poured down upon him, wave upon wave, from the hills. The Maxims were placed on the flanks of the brigade, and the batteries unlimbered and came into action at 1,200 yards range. Five minutes later Yakub, with the Khalifa's Black Flag, led 15,000 devoted fanatics against the isolated brigade. The Dervish onset was met by a hail of bullets and shells from 18 guns and 3,000 rifles, the Sudanese firing independently, and too fast for effect, the Egyptians in steady volleys.

When the European division, under General Gatacre, accompanied by the Sirdar, mounted the crest of the sandy ridge running down from Jebel Surgham, which stands 250 feet above the river, distant about a mile and a half, a hitherto sputtering fire from the hilltop increased in intensity, and the Sirdar ordered General Maxwell to "Change front to the right," and carry the hill. He sent orders to General Lewis to wheel to the right and come into line on Maxwell's right flank. He ordered General Lyttelton, with the 2nd Brigade, to form on General Maxwell's left, south of the Surgham hill; and Wauchope, with the 1st European Brigade, to hurry back and fill the wide gap, then nearly a mile, between Macdonald's left and Lewis's right; and sent the 32nd Battery to keep Macdonald going as fast as the teams could gallop. General Collinson's brigade and the Camel Corps were ordered to change front "three-quarters right about " to face towards Macdonald's right flank.

These movements, when executed, brought the army from its front to the south in echelon with its left on the river, and its right out in the desert to the westward, to facing west in line with its left in the desert, and its right nearly on the Nile, which there makes a bend inwards.

Maxwell's Sudanese scrambled up the rocks, and in spite of some fire cleared the peak with the bayonet, advancing over the western slope. Lewis came into action on Maxwell's right, and thus one British and two Egyptian brigades were firing on the right flank of the 15,000 men, who were streaming over the plain from the westward of Surgham hill to attack Macdonald. At this moment, except Wauchope's brigade, which was "doubling" in a north-westerly direction to Macdonald's assistance, and Collinson's Egyptian Brigade, which was still close to the river, the whole of the infantry and artillery were hotly engaged.

As the 7th Egyptian Battalion on the right of Lewis's brigade, the only corps commanded by a Native officer, deployed into line to lessen the gap between its brigade and that of Macdonald, the men became unsteady and fell back. General Archibald Hunter, who had joined Macdonald for a few moments, was now close to Lewis's brigade, and brought up two companies of the 15th Egyptian Battalion with fixed bayonets, and thus forced the 7th Battalion back into line. Henceforth it remained steady.

Yakub's warriors came on against Macdonald as bravely as any men ever ran to meet death on a battle-field, but the great wave of jibba-clad Dervishes was mowed down by the fire of rifles, and 26 guns under Macdonald's, besides those of Maxwell's and Lewis's commands.

Many of Yakub's bravest leaders fell dead, and his attack slackened. He and his bravest subordinates, disdaining death, perished where they stood beneath the Black Flag, and, though we are anticipating, we may now say that when their conquerors reached it the flag waved only over dead men.

Meanwhile Macdonald, after withstanding for nearly half an hour the onslaught of Yakub's devoted soldiers, had to meet a still more serious attack launched against the right and right rear of his brigade. He was facing south-west when he met Yakub's onslaught, and just as its vigour was lessening, two heavy columns attacked his right flank and right rear, led respectively by the Emirs All Wad Helu and Osman Sheikh Ed Din. Macdonald, who from private had risen to the rank of officer, was a great believer in square drill, and leaving the 2nd Battalion of Egyptians under command of Major Pink facing south-west, executed an old drill-book formation, "Prolong the line from the Left in succession by the rear to the Right," and so the 9th, 11th, and 10th Battalions now steadily changed their front, and from facing south-west formed a line facing north-west.

The change was effected only just in time, assisted a good deal by the remarkable steadiness of the 9th Battalion of Sudanese, which had been held in support behind the other three. The black soldier born in the Sudan has many fine qualities, but at the time of which we write he had not learnt the advantage of effective fire control. At the final charge each man had only three rounds left in hand; but, on the other hand, the blacks awaited with grinning faces the oncoming masses of Dervishes, with whom they wished to deal with the bayonet.

At this moment the Lincoln (10th) Regiment, which was the nearest of the four battalions of Wauchope's brigade, came up breathless, but at a steady double on the right of Macdonald's brigade, standing close to the 10th Sudanese, whom they termed "their black brothers". The steady volleys of the Lincoln Regiment materially thinned the ranks of Osman's oncoming masses, but not before some of his bravest followers were near enough to the line to throw their spears and wound some of our people.

It was now apparent, even to our heroic enemy, that the attack from the Kerreri Hills was half an hour too late. If it had been delivered simultaneously with that of Yakub's, Macdonald's brigade must have gone down, although they would probably have died on the ground where they stood. Five hundred Dervish horsemen, perceiving there was no hope of overcoming the British force, formed up about a quarter of a mile from the left of Macdonald's brigade. Many carried no weapons, but all, urging the horses to their utmost speed, rode without hesitation to certain death.

The whole fell dead under the fire of guns and rifles, a few riderless horses only breaking through the left of the brigade.

The battle was now over. The Dervishes, who had advanced with the greatest courage at sunrise, leaving 9,000 dead and vast numbers wounded, fled in utter confusion, pursued by the 21st Lancers and Egyptian cavalry and Camel Corps. There were rather over 2,000 corpses outside the zareba, which had been held by the whole army. There were 1,400 lying to the left front of Macdonald's first position, slain by his men and by Maxwell's and Lewis's brigades; while of those who descended from the Kerreri Hills and assailed Macdonald after the change of front, there were over 4,000 bodies.

The Sirdar accepted the surrender of the city that evening. The British Division had 175 casualties, including 14 officers; the Egyptian army 273, including 10 officers; and the Dervishes lost killed, 10,000 to 15,000 wounded.

From British Battles on Land and Sea by Field Marshal Sir Evelyn Wood (Cassell, 1915)

Chapter 7

The 2nd Devons at Bois Des Buttes, 1918

In March 1918 after three and a half years of gruelling effort the German army showed that although it had been pressed back it was by no means beaten. In a series of tremendous attacks it showed that it might still win the war. With great difficulty the first attacks were held but then, on 27 May, an even greater attack was launched. What happened at Bois des Buttes is described in a Corps Special Order which was signed by Major B. L. Montgomery. He was a staff officer with IX Corps at this stage in his distinguished career:

On 27th May, after the enemy had captured our forward and main defences the Second Devonshire Regiment maintained an unbroken front up to a late hour in the morning. Although surrounded and repeatedly attacked it successfully defeated all attempts of the enemy to advance on its front. The time thus gained was of the utmost value as it enabled the defences south west of the AISNE to be organised, and reinforcing troops to occupy the position unmolested.

A Battery commander who was on the spot states that at a late hour in the morning he found the Commanding officer of the Second Devonshire Regiment, and a handful of men, holding on to the last trench north of the Aisne. They were in a position where they were entirely without hope of help, but were fighting on grimly. The Commanding Officer himself was calmly writing his orders with a storm of H.E. shell falling round him. His magnificent bearing, dauntless courage, and determination to carry on to the end, were worthy of the highest admiration. There is no doubt that this Battalion perished en masse. It refused to surrender and fought to the last.

The Officer Commanding the Second Devonshire Regiment (Lt-Col R. H. Anderson-Morshead) together with 28 other officers and 552 other ranks, practically the whole battalion in the area north of the river AISNE, fought it out to the last as ordered.

The account which follows was written by the late Reginald A. Colwill who was with the 2nd Devons at the time. At the end of the war he felt that this feat of courage and endurance should be more widely known and published a book on it. He did this at his own expense, for at that time people wished to forget the war and had no desire to publish or read books about it.

The first part of the extract describes the regiment when it was resting in billets after previous battles; the second passage concerns the battle itself and is very much the fighting soldier's view. Its occasional incoherence is one of its more valuable features, for in a battle a man tends to notice occasional small details while not seeing the larger entity of which they are a part. Sometimes he clearly sees everyone and everything around him, and at other moments all he can visualize is what appears in the sights of his rifle.

IN BILLETS

Christmas, of the year 1917, saw the 2nd Battalion of the Devonshire Regiment enjoying a few days' rest at the little village of Setques, just a few kilometres behind St. Omer. They had deserved that short respite, for they had taken full share of the dirty work in the swamps of Flanders in the autumn, and it was like heaven itself to these hardworked, tired men to come back to the peace, and almost luxury, of a place where the only signs of war were the passing of troops towards the line, where an enemy aeroplane was not a too frequent visitor, and where work was not hard enough to create more than the usual grumble at having to do anything at all.

There was, too, the added luxury of baths, and at the paper mill down in the valley these soldiers were welcome visitors. They sat about in the warm rooms during the cold afternoons, and from the well into which the exhaust steam was pumped they drew an unlimited supply of hot water for the thorough cleansing of their underclothing.

They were not long here, but it was long enough to put fresh life into them. New drafts had arrived from home, bringing out some of the men who had been with the Battalion before, but more who were to have their first taste of war. It was all very queer to these newcomers. They had imagined the army in the field to be a dirty and more or less ragged army. They had certainly not looked for polishing and shining, for the Quarter-master-Sergt., with that great foresight which the Army displayed about little things right to the end of the war, had taken from them all their cleaning gear. It was something of a surprise to these men, then, when they found that the army in the field was looking far more presentable than were they themselves, who had only been in the country for a few days. And they were far from pleased when, out of the five francs paid them on the first pay-day after their arrival, they had to provide themselves with cleaning brushes, bianco and metal polish, charged for at the usual fancy prices at the little shops in the village.

But they were Devons. They had been taught at the depot of the 3rd Battalion, in Devonport, what it was to be smart. At the depot a man was doomed to almost permanent "C.B.," for by the time he had applied the daily coat of bianco to his web straps, and had completed the polishing of his brasses, and the cleaning of his rifle, it was time to go to bed. In the winter he had to do most of this work at his own expense, because there was not a gas fitting at Raglan Barracks which gave light enough to enable him to see what he was doing, and he had to provide his own candles for the purpose of illumination.

That was a peculiar little way of these Devons. They fought like demons when there was fighting to be done, but they hated the thought of it all the time and, like most of the troops, grumbled incessantly. They openly called the Devonshire Regiment and all its officers every objectionable name they could think of, but, privately, to their closest chums, they would confide their deepest admiration of the Devons and the men who led them. Let a half-drunken man of some other regiment say anything which, in the slightest degree, reflected on the Devons, and he was sure of the soundest hiding he had ever imagined.

There were men in the ranks of the Devons who were able to put two and two together and make four of them with just as much certainty as the officers over them. In this great Citizen Army there were many men of intelligence holding humble positions and some men with little intelligence in places of responsibility,

These men, who had left big businesses, and banks, and offices, and colleges, used to gather together to talk. There was no sort of snobbery about it, yet some of these men used to like to chat about literature, and music, and art. They liked, sometimes, to meet kindred spirits, and, during this hour of letter writing, without design or arrangement, they used to rub shoulders in this little room.

As they ate their chocolate, or drank their tea, before going home, they used to analyse the situation.

AT BOIS DES BUTTES

Nine o'clock was fixed for the departure of the first company. Just before that hour there marched up to the Headquarters a batch of men who had just arrived from the base. They included some men rejoining from hospitals, and some others who had never heard a gun fired or seen a German. They were at once divided among the companies, and within half-an-hour or so they were marching up with the others.

Six hours later many of them were killed and the others were wounded and in the hands of the enemy.

The Adjutant, Capt. U. B. Burke, hurried forward before the companies took over the position, looking out, as well as he was able, the trenches they were to occupy.

The Battalion was nominally in reserve. They were posted in tunnels cut through two little hills - technically known as "pimples" - in the Bois des Buttes, about three quarters of a mile behind the front line trenches, immediately in front of Juvincourt, and to the left of the road - looking towards the line - connecting Juvincourt with Roucy. Another road, connecting Pontavert and Berry-au-Bac, formed a triangle of the piece of land on the right of the Juvincourt road.

Woods covered these "pimples", low brush wood extended out in front of them for some distance on the level, and flat woods were on the other side of the road. Everywhere the grass and herbage stood high, hiding wire entanglements in many cases, though others stood out clear enough. The trenches which were supposed to exist in front of the hills amounted to little when it came to defensive work. They were all in bad condition, and the field of fire was nowhere of great use. Away on the left, the line was being held by the 5th Division.

As the companies marched up our own artillery was getting active. The men behind the lines heard the guns and imagined the enemy was coming over. But they were wrong. The Germans were only firing an occasional round, at nothing in particular. They were probably only firing to cover other noises which might have given an alarm, had it not already been given. From 9.45 p.m. onwards, our guns were increasingly active. Then a few gas shells were sent over by the enemy. Not a lot, but one now and again.

Then quietness. More shelling, and another period of quiet. Then not a sound. There was something uncanny about it. Way down in those deep dug-outs the men were finding corners to rest their equipment. Some of them were asking anxiously when they would be put in the trenches. Callous "old sweats", unconsciously prophetic, did their best to add to the discomfort of the youngsters by telling them they would be "blown to hell before break-fast".

In Brigade Headquarters, close at hand, they were talking over the 'phone to the front line. Everything was quiet there. The trenches had not been shelled at all. There was no rifle fire all along the front.

From the moment when Brigadier-General Grogan walked into the headquarters of the 2nd Devons, at Roucy, and gave orders for the Battalion to move into the line at once, there had been no opportunity for Lieut.-Col. Anderson-Morshead to discuss the matter with the company commanders, for they had only just time to get ready to move in order to get their companies away according to plan. Now, however, there was a moment. Word had been passed round that each company was to send down to the dump for more ammunition, though there had not been time for these orders to be carried out. Then the Commanding Officer sent for all company commanders to attend a conference in the Battalion Headquarter dug-out, deep down below a pill-box under what was known as the Wagner Redoubt.

Here he explained the situation as well as he was able to do, for his own information was not too extensive. He told them that an attack was expected that morning at one o'clock. It was then P-tn., so they had not long to wait. He recounted to them the French instructions that not a foot of ground was to be surrendered and that they were to hold on at all costs. The positions of the companies had already been explained to them.

The conference was over. It was a hot night and the atmosphere below ground was sultry. The commanders were about to file out when the Colonel, with consideration for others which was one of his strong characteristics, suggested a drink. A bottle of whiskey was forthcoming, but there was only one glass. There was a general laugh over this, but nobody was prepared to be exacting, and a drink was welcome.

"How quiet it all is!" observed the Commanding Officer, as the last of the party was draining the glass to its last drop. "Damnably quiet. Not even a rifle shot. Probably all 'wind-up' again!"

He glanced at his wristlet watch as he spoke. The dial showed him that it was exactly one o'clock. Two dull thuds. Gas shells. Then a mighty roar.

The hour had struck. Two thousand guns crashed out in chorus. The whole earth shook. Hell was let loose. Never had there before, in the world's history, been such a cannonade.

Above their heads, shells screamed. Our own artillery was answering with all their power, but what a little echo compared with that mass of guns on the other side!

At that moment the fatigue parties were starting out to fetch the ammunition. But they never got beyond the entrances to the dug-outs. It was impossible for anybody to move in the trenches and live. They kept inside the entrances and waited for a chance which never came. Some of them were caught in the avalanche of steel and cut to bits.

Then the sweet, nauseating smell of gas. More high explosive, and more and more gas. A dash was made to fix the gas curtains. Blankets were stretched across the entrances to the dug-outs. No air could get in. But there was enough gas in the tunnels to make it perilous to be there unprotected, and so gas masks were put on.

There, underground, it was insufferable. The night was unbearably hot, the men had been marching hard, they were crowded together in small spaces, and with all air shut out their condition was terrible.

Still it was better there than it would have been outside, for it seemed that the enemy was shelling those woods in particular. Perhaps he was. Perhaps every spot was getting the same attention. He had enough guns going to make life impossible anywhere on the front.

No news was coming through to the Regiment. The Brigade got a few messages, early, to say that the front line was receiving a terrible time, but that no attempt had yet been made to rush the trenches. Then all was silence. Nobody knew what was happening up in front. As a matter of fact, with the first rounds the enemy had put shells into the trenches. Most of the entrances to the dug-outs, the position of every one of which he knew, were closed by dropping shells in front of them. The men who were below ground in numbers of cases perished where they were.

And what of the artillery? The batteries had taken up positions vacated by the French. Unknown to the British artillery officers, these positions had remained unchanged for a whole year. The Germans had the bearings, and the range, of every gun. With their first shot, they silenced many of them. Every gun was put out of action, or its crew killed, within a few hours.

That was why the men in the dug-outs, waiting for the order to get into their trenches, wondered what was happening to our artillery. They were no longer an effective protection for the infantry, though here and there a few guns still managed to keep going for some time yet.

It seemed an interminable time of waiting down below ground. Two o'clock came, half-past two, three. Still no news from the front. There never was any more news.

At the first peep of daylight, Col. Anderson-Morshead decided to wait no longer. He ordered the companies out into the open. "B" Company he placed in charge of Lieut. F. D. Clarke, M.C. Lieut. T. Oreton, having been delayed, could not start for the line till midnight and, with Capt. G. O. Openshaw, got caught in the barrage. Capt. Openshaw was apparently killed on the road - as a matter of fact he was seriously wounded and died later, in Germany — but Lieut. Oreton afterwards played his part in the retirement. His company — "B" — was on the extreme left, facing Laon, with the 50th Division on their left. "C" and "D" Companies, commanded respectively, by Lieut. Tindal and Lieut. F. E. Flarris, were employed further on the light. They took up positions as near to the edge of the wood as they could get, and were, more or less, astride the road, "C" Company being on the extreme right. "A" Company, and Battalion Headquarters manned the trenches round the sides of the hill under which the dug-outs were constructed.

Still the hellish gunfire continued. The trenches were, in most places, blown flat. In no case was there more than a few yards standing. Even getting into position, several men were lost and others were wounded and sent to find their ways back to headquarters and the aid post. Though only a few yards in rear, few of them got as far.

From his headquarters on the little hill, the Colonel could see nothing of the companies. He very soon sent runners out - two going together — to each company to learn whether they were in their positions. They never reached the companies. Signallers were useless. They could not keep any lines standing for five minutes in such a barrage. No army had ever imagined such gunfire, bad as it had been in many previous battles. The companies had gone out and were, to all intents, lost.

Every dawn on that front, up to now, had been gloriously clear. There had not been a morning mist since the troops had been here. But the Germans had their usual luck. This morning there was a heavy white haze. The hills above Roucy stood out clear, when the sun came up, but here on the flat land, beyond the river, the haze hung thick and low. Added to it, was the smoke of the shelling and the dust. It was practically impossible to see anything.

Still the Colonel got no news. But the enemy infantry had made their attack at 3.45 a.m. Col. Anderson-Morshead sent across to Brigade Headquarters. It had moved, and he was left without any information, could see nothing and could not find what had happened to his companies.

The Brigade had got its first information as to what was going on from the Brigade Intelligence Officer. He had first reported that the mist had prevented anything being seen. Then he wired back that the enemy observation balloons were going up where our front line had been.

A little later, and Division had news that the enemy was advancing down the line of the Miette River, which joins the Aisne midway between Pontavert and Berry-au-Bac. That meant that he was advancing towards the rear of the Devons, on their right. Then another wire, to the effect that the Germans were through the 50th Division on the left, and marching towards the Ville au Bois.

But no news of any attack on the front, although the enemy was well through on each flank, and already surrounding the Devons. Col. Anderson-Morshead never had any of these messages. He did not know that his companies were already engaged with the enemy, and were fighting, not to keep him back only, but for their very lives, against such odds as men were never called upon to face before in all war's ghastly history. How should he know? With all that din, a little more or less would pass unnoticed.

The front lines had been laid almost flat an hour before. Little 118 parties were holding out there. Some were surrounded, and still fought on. Among them were the West Yorks and Middlesex. They sent out pigeon messages asking for help. Help! Dear Lord, where was help to come from? There was no help to give, and if there had been it could never have been got to them. It was not possible for anything to stand beyond the skirt of the wood and live. Down in the dug-out the Medical Officer, Lieut. H. F. Kane, M.C., - one of the first Americans in the war - was surrounded by hopeless cases.

Other little parties, driven out of their trenches, were fighting their way back. And the Germans, in thousands, were hurrying their retreat and wiping them out. As they came over in waves, they threw bombs down the dug-outs and passed on.

It was "B" Company which first engaged the enemy. He came through quicker on the left. The men had hardly found places from which they could get a field of fire. The mist still hung low and they could see nothing that was not right on them. What chance had they then?

It is Corpl. L. Leat, of "B" Company, who gives the best account of the enemy's method of attack. At the outset he could see little, but he had a clear recollection of it when interrogated by the writer just after the armistice. While he was dodging about on the front of the wood for an hour, a very vivid mental picture was formed.

"When the barrage lifted," he said, "we saw the Germans coming in long lines, one close behind the other. They were not more than 500 yards from us, coming over our old front line trenches. Behind their lines we could see them in dense numbers, bringing down the road all sorts of transport and guns. Away over on the right, two tanks were lumbering along, and, attached to a chain which joined them, was a captive observation balloon, following close behind the infantry. Three aeroplanes flew over us and deluged us with machine-gun bullets. The barrage was still getting us in our positions, though a good deal of it had lifted and had been thrown further back. We could see the enemy coming for miles behind his lines.

"We had two Lewis guns, and these opened fire, sweeping down great numbers of Germans, while the men in the trenches maintained rapid fire continuously at the waves and waves of the enemy who still continued to approach. In their front wave they had rifle men. These approached to within nearly fifty yards of our trenches and then took cover. From somewhere behind their first wave there was another which bombed us with rifle grenades, and, after this had continued for some time, during which we had suffered heavy casualties, the rifle men, who had been taking cover and getting ready for the assault, suddenly jumped up and rushed at us.

"The boys kept blazing away and this attack was beaten off, but they had hardly given a sign of falling back before the rifle grenades came falling among us, doing even greater damage than before.

"Then a third party of Germans attacked us, coming forward through the rifle grenadiers and the rifle men, and hurling stick bombs into our trench. There were hundreds of them, and, though we took a heavy toll, they also had their revenge, and our ranks were thinned out terribly."

How could men stand against this sort of thing? Yet stand they did, though shells made further breaches in the trenches and separated the men and smashed up any sort of line there had ever been. Men lost touch with their officers. Officers were killed. N.C.O.'s took charge. The N.C.O.'s were casualties, and private soldiers - young private soldiers, seventeen-and-a-half years old, some of them, in their first fight - took command and did gallant things.

This little extract from the last letter sent to his father by Private A. J. Borne, a lad of twenty, who died in hospital just after his repatriation as a prisoner of war: "I was," he wrote, "with the Lewis gun team, and we were first in action. All my pals of the team were speedy casualties, including Gennoe and Roberts. Lads were falling right and left, but I had a capital weapon in the Lewis gun, which I was firing steadily at the German hordes. I looked about, and I seemed to be all alone. Still, I kept on firing at them. Then, when the enemy waves were about a hundred yards away, things got a bit too warm, so I picked up the gun, ran back about a hundred yards, and had another go."

All alone . . . running back and having another go. That boy was fighting like that for three hours before he was a casualty.

Time was passing. The aeroplanes were getting more and more active. Not only were they machine-gunning the defenders, but they were spotting for the artillery, and many a well-directed shell took its terrible toll. Corpl. L. S. Wotton, of No. 7 Platoon, for instance, relates an incident which is not without its humorous side. Humour amidst such ghastly tragedy! He tells how the enemy machine-gun fire became so intensive that it was impossible for a man to put his head up without being hit. An aeroplane came over and they fired at it, so low was the aviator. They failed to bring him down, but he turned and went back. Corpl. Wotton goes on: "The 'plane had hardly got out of sight before our bit of cover was being shelled. We then moved further back, and still this 'plane came and went back as before. More shells. Next time it came we waited till it turned to go back and tell where we were. Then we quickly changed our position, and when the next lot of shells dropped we were not there to get them. We had spoiled him nicely!"

If you had known the spirit of those men, you would realise that they laughed when those shells fell in the wrong place. That was the spirit which made it possible for men to do the things they did. Things anybody would consider to be impossible.

The Colonel had long ago realised that the first runners sent out to the companies would never come back. He knew what had happened to them. He then sent out Capt. J. Milner, M.C., the assistant adjutant, in company with another runner, to see if he could get any information. Capt. Milner accomplished his mission. And what a scene of horror met his eyes everywhere. Men fighting for dear life. The ground all churned up. Dead and dying and horribly mutilated forms everywhere. "B" Company had practically disappeared. He saw the other two companies holding their battered trenches. It took him a long time to get back. Before he got there other things had happened. The enemy, who had broken through on the left, were working round behind the hills. Lieut. Maunder was sent up with the Headquarter Company to reinforce the front line. He had hardly started when he met little remnants coming back. They told him there was no front line; that the enemy was pressing hard behind them, and that they had had orders to fall back. He took over these men and formed another line on the side of the hill. With wonderful pluck, despite what they had been through, these lads manned the parapet again, and where there was no parapet stretched out on the ground and waited for the enemy, who was not long in coming.

Lieut. Clarke tried to get back with No. 6 Platoon, but had great difficulty in finding his way. He at last struck the tunnel and when he came out at the other side he was assailed with bullets from every direction. He managed to cross the bridge with a mere handful of men and played a further part for many days after. He was the only officer who escaped. Lieut. R. F. B. Hill, with another platoon - or the three remaining men of a platoon - was less lucky. They had run out of ammunition and ran into a big body of enemy before they reached the bridge. They were captured.

On the hill, looking through his glasses, the Colonel was searching to see what was going on in front. But the smoke hid everything. The machine-gunning was getting fiercer and closer. Bullets were flying thickly round, but the enemy could not be seen. He was coming through the companies. Capt. Milner had not returned, so L/Corpl. W. H. Jordan, the Colonel's personal orderly, was sent to tell the companies to move back to intermediate trenches. He went off with another runner, Pte. Staddon, to fulfil this perilous mission. Nobody really ever expected them to accomplish it, or to see them again.

Looking away to the right, Capt. Burke noticed numbers of stragglers of other regiments making for Pontavert as hard as their exhausted state would allow them. He sent a corporal to tell them to join the Devons. They declined to join the Devons, or anybody else. They had had enough of it. They were going back.

Poor devils! They were but human; they had been through more than human flesh and blood could stand. It is doubtful whether any but the very earliest to start ever got away, for the enemy was pouring through on the right, and probably cut off their retreat.

While all this was going on, "C" and "D" Companies were being hotly attacked in much the same way that "B" had been. There were a few tanks which chased them, there were the same waves of rifle men, grenadiers and hand bombers. After the battle the ground was covered thickly with stick-bombs, and how a single man ever escaped with his life must for ever remain a mystery. Not only did the aeroplanes use machine-guns, but they bombed and dropped aerial torpedos. There must have been tons of the latter dropped on three or four square miles that morning.

What daring acts of bravery, what acts of heroism were performed there on the right, as well as on the left. It is difficult to collate everything in its proper order. It is impossible to do so. But there were some things which must be placed on record. There was the gallantry of Lieut. Tindal - quiet, firm, brave Lieut. Tindal, a man loved by every man in the Battalion, a man any soldier who knew him would have died to save. All the morning he calmly directed his men in "C" Company. Sergt. Harry Cosway, D.C.M., tells the thrilling story of his death.

They were, he said, in an old German trench, too deep to enable them to defend it well. Parties were sent out to try to get into touch with the 24th Brigade, stated to be on their right. Meanwhile wounded of the West Yorks and Middlesex were coming back from the front line. The enemy had not broken through then. Later, the parties which had gone out in search of the 24th Brigade came back and reported that they could find no trace of them. An hour later considerable numbers of the West Yorks and Middlesex came through and reported that their regiments had been blown to pieces and had sustained terrible losses. Numbers of these men were wounded, and all were very exhausted.

Lieut. Tindal then held a hurried conference with his officers and N.C.O.'s. Among the others were Capt. G. A. Miller, Lieut. F. C. Leat, Sergts. Cosway, Bates and Pile.

"He told us," said Sergt. Cosway, "that he had decided to stay in that position at all costs. He told us that he had received no orders to retire, and should not do so. We agreed, if necessary, to fight to the last man."

How nobly they kept that promise! Not a man fell back!

The next news was that the enemy was approaching in great numbers on the right. It will be recollected that it was on the right that he first broke the line, near Berry-au-Bac. In view of this knowledge, the company was changed over to a trench which ran parallel with the road to Juvincourt, and which faced Berry- au-Bac. The news was that there was, at least, a battalion of Germans advancing on this company — this very thin company - and the news proved to be an under-estimate rather than an over-estimate. They were coming round to try to take the company in the rear, for the flank was in the air.

Let Sergt. Cosway continue the story: "Lieut. Tindal ordered us to fix bayonets and get ready to charge. We now saw the enemy in tremendous force, and it seemed, from the very start, to be a hopeless thing to charge them. But we had been put there to check the advance, and this appeared the only way to do it. They were almost on us before we had a chance to use the rifle to any extent, but we managed to inflict terrible damage on them. We had one Lewis gun and, until it was put out of action with a hand grenade, L/Corpl. Hannaford used it to good purpose."

The company had been divided into two sections, in order that one lot could fire from another trench, and, soon after this division had been made, Lieut. Tindal decided that the moment had arrived for a charge. On his shout the men climbed over the low parapet and, with a wild yell, dashed on the enemy.

What was left of half a company — certainly not more than twenty men - charging a battalion of German!

But they never came to grips. After going a few yards they found themselves hung up on a lot of old, low, barbed-wire entanglements, hidden in the undergrowth, and the presence of which nobody suspected. The enemy raked them with machine- gun and rifle fire.

They dropped prone in front of the wire and took what cover they could in shell holes. Here they were deluged with stick- bombs. Still the men who were not hit continued to reply with a vigorous rifle fire, and many men who were wounded still managed to get the rifle to their shoulders and pull the triggers. Ammunition was getting short, as the men only had what was in their pouches, and there was no means of getting any more. The ranks were being fast wiped out. The Germans were creeping closer and closer, Lieut. Tindal was lying near Sergt. Bates. The latter had just fired at a German officer. "You've missed him, Bates. Leave him to me," said Lieut. Tindal. He raised himself on his left arm and took aim with his revolver. Before he could fire, a bullet had struck him in the head. Thus died a gallant officer.

Lieut. Leat took charge and showed great bravery, making fine use of a rifle. It was only a matter of minutes after that he followed his company commander with a bullet through the head.

Then, with eight men left out of fifty, Sergt. Cosway carried on.

Every man was a hero, but certainly Pte. D. Greenslade added laurels to his M.M. During the assault of "C" Company a German machine-gun was doing great damage. Pte. Greenslade worked himself into a position where he could command the gun, though he could not see it. He let off five rounds rapid. The gun stopped. He had probably hit the gunner. After a pause it started again, firing at point blank range of not more than a hundred yards. Pte. Greenslade let go another ten rounds rapid, and the gun was silenced. Then he crawled in the trench again, to continue to fight with the others.

Half-a-dozen men, separated from the rest, lay stretched on the ground, without a bit of cover, blazing away at the approaching Germans in the face of a perfect hail of fire. They were all killed where they lay. It was a mere incident, but a glorious one. Nobody knows who they were.

Then there was another brave machine-gunner. Pte. H. G. Budge, also of "C" Company. He set up his Lewis gun and kept it working with his gun crew. Finally the enemy tried to rush him.

He sent his crew back, but kept firing away in the face of a mass of Germans. Then, when they were just about to pounce upon him, he put his gun out of action.

By this time, both "C" and "D" Companies were absolutely surrounded and there were Germans everywhere - thousands of them. The Devons in the forward area - in fact all the Devons - were caught like rats in a trap. Pte. M. Knight, of "C" Company, and five other men in a bit of old trench, entirely separated from all the others, found themselves being approached on all sides. Gallantly they stood in a rough circle, back to back, blazing away for very life. And even then they fought their way out, and set up a further defence in another bit of trench further back!

Before passing on to see what the other companies were doing, an account of a fine bit of heroism, contributed by Pte. G. T. Chuter, must be set down. There must have been many such acts, but there is no record of them. At the time of which he speaks, "C" Company had been reduced to twenty men, under Capt. Miller. They went over the top with the idea of charging the enemy, but found that they were so hopelessly outnumbered that Capt. Miller thought they would do better work in the trench, so ordered them back again. The Germans were closing in on them. There was one Lewis gun remaining. This was in charge of Pte. Cakebread. L/Corpl. Cox, who also had knowledge of the Lewis gun, assisted the gunner. "These two men," says Pte. Chuter, "made up their minds that if they moved away to the right they could bring a much more deadly fire to bear on the enemy, although in so doing they placed themselves under direct fire from the Germans, as no cover was available. It is my firm conviction that these two men placed themselves in this hazardous position for the benefit of the few of us who were left. We remonstrated with them, trying to point out the extreme peril of what they proposed doing, but they would not be turned from their plan. They were successful in reaching the position, and we heard the gun firing. Then, after a while, it stopped. Later, both their bodies were found beside the gun."

But that heroism allowed the remnant of "C" Company to hold their position for another twenty minutes.

While all these heroic deeds were being performed by "C" Company, "D" Company, adjoining, was having just as awful a time. It was before four o'clock, according to Sergt. C. S. Hooper, D.C.M., that he discovered that Germans were already in one end of a piece of trench that "D" Company was holding. This party of the Devons were fortunate in having a number of bombs with them, and by making good use of these, and finally charging with bayonets, they drove the enemy out, taking possession of the trench themselves.

Then the Germans came again, with stick-bombs and hand grenades, causing a lot of casualties, till at last things began to look so bad that the Devons gave up the trench and the Germans occupied it for the second time. About a dozen men who remained bombed the Germans out and reoccupied the trench once more, but a second time they were blown out of it. For a third time the little party attacked the Germans, and once more gained possession of the trench. This time the enemy not only drove them out again, but a bomb from an aeroplane blew the trench up completely. The survivors were scattered, dodging here and there, escaping death by a miracle from hand grenades, bombs, and machine-gun bullets from the air as well as the land.

Lieut. F. E. Harris, of the 2nd Rhodesian Regiment, who had been transferred to the Devons, and who was affectionately referred to by the men of the Company as " the Rhodesian officer " - few of them knowing his name - was an inspiration to the men. There is a typical reference to him in the account by Pte. J. H. Hinckley, who says: "The most conspicuous man there was the South African Lieutenant. By his encouraging words and behaviour, he seemed to put heart into us, and we greatly needed it at the time, for we saw the other Divisions retiring in the distance, and we knew we had to hold on to let them get back far enough to establish fresh positions."

Lieut. Harris evidently succeeded in putting heart into his men, for "D" Company held on grandly. This officer admired his Devonshire soldiers and his Commanding Officer. When an aeroplane came over, flying particularly low, he jumped on the top of the trench and, pointing up at the 'plane, called on the men to shoot at it.

As he did so, the machine-gunner in the 'plane let rip and slightly scratched the officer's arm. Strange as it may seem, he remarked, "I believe the beggar did it on purpose!" This man who could joke in the face of death! Was it any wonder his example inspired the men?

Another officer who was popular with the Company was Lieut. C. E. Pells. He had, in his heart, bitter hatred for the Germans, for his only child was drowned when they sank the Lusitania. And all that morning he seemed to take fiendish delight in mowing them down with a rifle. He moved about, cheering the men and showing them how to take better cover. Then he was killed.

Lieut. Harris sent out to find out what support he had. It was a sorry tale the men brought back, for, somehow, they managed to get back. They told him Lieut. Tindal had been killed, and that "C" Company was practically wiped out. They told him that his other flank was in the air. Still they fought on, knowing that nothing could save them.

L/Sergt. R. Bradford tells of the bravery of Lieut. A. E. Ruttledge. The Lieutenant thought his party could do better work by getting on the road and attempting to stop the Germans coming down. They got there, and Lieut. Ruttledge, without any regard for his personal safety, ran here and there finding better positions for the young soldiers, who had no experience of battle, cheering them on and telling them what to do. He fought desperately with every kind of weapon he could lay hands on. Lieut. Harris had been severely wounded and was thought to be dead. As a matter of fact he recovered consciousness a week later, a prisoner of war.

So the battle waged. All the time surrounded, dodging here and there, killing and being killed, doing their best to stem the advance of the enemy, hoping all the time that their sacrifice would mean something to the men behind. The last word of "D" Company speaks of Lieut. Ruttledge and four men remaining fighting desperately in a little bit of trench near the edge of the wood.

The forward companies had wonderfully upheld the most glorious traditions of the Regiment. And over all the scene of horror and desolation, over the sight of a tom earth, of men ripped and mutilated beyond recognition, God's glorious sun was shining. The mockery of it all!

All these things which have been described were happening simultaneously. All the companies were involved in the same attack, though it seems that "B" Company was the first to come to actual grips. And it was not very long before the attack on the forward companies started that the Headquarters and "A" Companies, on the little hills behind, were engaged. It might have been an hour or so before they were actually in the thick of the fighting, but as soon as the Germans had overwhelmed the companies in front of the wood they left ample force to deal with them and pushed on. Let us now follow what was going on at headquarters, remembering that, from time to time, as they lost touch with their comrades, men from "B", "C", and "D" Companies dribbled back to take their stand with the others who remained.

The last time we saw what was happening with headquarters was when the Colonel sent out L/Corpl. Jordan, in company with another runner, Pte. Staddon, to see what was happening in front of the wood. He had sent out other runners, who were killed, and Capt. Milner, who had not then returned.

All this time Lieut. Maunder's party was being hotly assailed and gradually it became only too evident that the enemy had got round their left flank. As a matter of fact, under cover of the woods, the invaders who broke through the 50th Division had worked right round the bottom of the hill and, when the defenders were driven to the top of it, they found themselves being shot at from all angles.

Then L/Corpl. Jordan returned, and it was a tragic story he had to give the Commanding Officer. He recounted that "B" Company had been wiped out altogether, and that "C" and "D" Companies could not be expected to last very much longer. The barrage from the artillery had lifted from the hills now, and was being concentrated on the areas further back. The Germans were marching in column of fours down the road from Berry-au- Bac, and their transport was also passing through Pontavert, over a mile behind. They had set up machine guns on the outskirts of that village and were shooting down stragglers and walking wounded who were trying to make their way back to the aid posts.

The machine-guns were getting closer. Many of them had come through the companies in front and were setting up their guns in the wood at the foot of the hills, firing through the leaves which, on that spring morning, fell as though the frost had gripped them before an autumn gale. The branches were being stripped by bullets.

Col. Anderson-Morshead looked very grave, but there was fixed determination in every line of his face. The 2nd Devons, he knew, he could rely on. He knew that few, if any, of them would ever see another sun rise. For himself, he never had a feeling, but those who have fought with him know how he loved his men, and his heart must have been bleeding at the thought of all that ghastly slaughter, especially when he must have realised the utter futility of the mad orders he had been set to carry out. But Lieut. Col. Anderson-Morshead was every inch a soldier. He had been told to stand to the last man; his job was to hold up the enemy as much as possible, to allow those who managed to get across the bridge, beyond Pontavert, to make another line and fight again.

Quickly, but without any panic, he got all the men together and took them to another position on the back of the mound. Here they found themselves under a perfect rain of machine-gun fire and men were getting knocked out at an alarming rate. It was now about half-past eight in the morning. The Germans had been round the back of the hill in force for a full hour.

A move was made to other trenches. The party was divided. The Colonel took charge of one section - on the right - Lieut. W. L. Barrett was in command of another - on the left - and Capt. Burke remained with another which stayed on the front of the hill. By this arrangement, they were covering three sides of the hill. Capt. Burke, the hero of many a fight, and whose reputation in the Battalion was that there was no task too hazardous to set him to do, was an inspiration to his men. He worked like a demon. All the morning he had been dashing about getting information about the general situation. Once he got as far as Pontavert, and there was shot at, point blank, by the Germans already in possession. It was he who told the Colonel that the retreat to the bridge had been cut off. Knowing that, he still went coolly about directing fire. A great soldier, Capt. Burke! From these new trenches, there was a much better field of fire, and the men made the best use of their opportunities. They shot down Germans by the score. Indeed, there were so many of the enemy, everywhere, by this time that it would have been difficult to fire in any direction without hitting them. The party was getting smaller and smaller, and every man who was hit had to be left where he fell. Nobody could stop to give him attention, for it was all the survivors could do to hold the attackers off.

Col. Anderson-Morshead had just told the men that their last chance of escape had gone. He explained to them that the bridge was taken, and that the village of Pontavert was swarming with the enemy. "Your job for England, men," he said, "is to hold the blighters up as much as you can, to give our troops a chance on the other side of the river. There is no hope of relief. We have to fight to the last."

How cool he was is shown by the following statement, made by an artillery officer who was escaping with his gunners, their battery having been destroyed and the men being unarmed. It has been quoted in nearly every account which has appeared of this epic stand of the 2nd Devons, and this record would be incomplete without it. He wrote:

"At a later hour of the morning, I, with those of my men who had escaped the enemy machine guns and his fearful barrage, found the Commanding officer of the 2nd Devonshire Regiment and a handful of men holding on to the last trench north of the canal. They were in a position in which they were entirely without hope of help, but were fighting on grimly.

"The Commanding Officer himself was calmly writing his notes with a perfect hail of H.E. - high explosive - falling round him. I spoke to him, and he told me that nothing could be done. He refused all offers of help from my artillery men, who were unarmed, and sent them off to get through if they could. His magnificent courage, dauntless bearing and determination to carry on to the end moved one's emotion."

Capt. Milner had come back by now, and was taking his part in the defence. He and Capt. Burke, together with R.S.M. Frank Radford, were moving about, shouting words of encouragement, and the men responded by firing more rapidly than before. Their "Well done, lad!" meant a lot to those men. It was good to go into the presence of their Maker with words of earthly commendation still ringing in their ears.

The Colonel also kept moving about, closely followed by his orderly, L/Corpl. Jordan. The orderly looked towards Pontavert, and there saw the enemy transport on the road. Glancing in the other direction, he saw the Germans advancing in columns down the road from Juvincourt, with guns and transport. He pointed them out to the Colonel, who, in the midst of all that butchery, in the face of immediate death, calmly took his pipe from his pocket, remarking as he filled it, without a trace of emotion in his voice, "Ah well, Jordan, we shall have to make the best of it!"

Certain death, and they would make the best of it!

There were less than fifty men remaining now. Six hours before there had been 600 of them, all told.

From Through Hell to Victory: From Passchendaele to Mons with the 2nd Devons in 1918 (R. A. Colwill, 1927)

Chapter 8

The Punjabis

In their three-hundred-year stay on the Indian sub-continent the British fought many hard battles but also created many Indian army units which subsequently fought with great distinction in other countries. Of British officers with such regiments it was often said 'the regiment is his life', and many would not marry until the time came for them to retire. Members of these regiments, whatever their rank, felt that they were members of a family and were as keen as their officers and NCOs to reach a high standard of efficiency. Such a regiment was the Punjabis, who were formed in 1857.

They fought with verve and distinction on the North-West Frontier, in China, in East Africa in the First World War and in Burma in the Second. This account of an action in Burma is written by an officer who joined the regiment in 1938. The unit concerned was the 1st/16th Punjabis.

In November, as the Japanese started to secure jumping-off places for their coming spring offensive, the 1st/16th fought its first major engagement. The Japanese 33rd Division had begun to close in on the region round Tiddim in the Chin Hills some 160 miles south of Imphal. A single infantry brigade of the 17th Division was responsible for that sector of the front and it called urgently for help. The 1st/16th was sent to its assistance. The Battalion took up a position on a ridge some 8,000 feet high and almost twenty miles from Tiddim. Here, on a cold autumn night, the Japanese attacked. They assaulted the face of the position, but these attacks were held. They also climbed on to the ridge behind it and attacked from the rear. As the dawn broke, hordes of Japanese infantry came charging down on the thinly held trenches; they crashed through to Battalion Headquarters, but Lieutenant-Colonel Wilcock, now the commanding officer, improvised a line of signallers and orderlies and checked their advance. The Japanese called for artillery fire. Colonel Wilcock, sitting on his shooting-stick in the open, was killed almost immediately; the adjutant died beside him. The line was shattered and the Japanese poured on to the crest. A hastily organized counterattack failed to dislodge them. Now the Battalion faced a difficult situation. The Japanese held the top of the ridge, the key to the position, in strength, and had overrun the area containing the reserve ammunition; 'B' and 'D' Companies were being closely pressed. The second-in-command, Major Newell, resolved to break contact and rejoin the main body of the Brigade in the neighbourhood of Tiddim.

Jettisoning everything that could not be carried on the man, the Battalion struck out through virgin jungle. After two days threading their way across the steep slopes of the Chin Hills the tired men managed to rejoin the Brigade. The Japanese made no attempt to exploit their success.

The 1st/16th had suffered only some seventy casualties and had been manoeuvred rather than driven off its position; as a baptism of fire it had been a bitter experience and the loss of Colonel Wilcock, who knew every man in the Battalion and enjoyed their unquestioning trust, was a heavy blow; it was not to be forgotten or forgiven.

After two more months holding positions about Tiddim, the Battalion returned to its own brigade in the Imphal plateau. In the new year it carried out a month of intensive training, putting into practice all it had learned in the Chin Hills. When the crunch came in May 1944, and 4 Corps on the Imphal plain was surrounded, it was trained, fit and ready.

During the long-drawn-out battle that followed, it operated as often as not behind the enemy lines. As regards uniform and equipment at this time, the 1st/16th wore olive-green bush shirts and olive-green trousers tucked into the standard short gaiter and boots; the men wore the normal equipment but the heavy and clumsy pack was put aside and replaced by the haversack carried well up the back between the shoulders. The cardigan was rolled inside the gas cape, the lightweight waterproof cape that had a hundred uses besides protection against gas, the whole being fastened to the waistbelt by straps taken from the pack. In the haversack the men carried three days' lightscale rations (these were later replaced by the American 'K5 ration). The sepoys, of course, could not eat bully beef and were given tinned sardines or herrings instead. The waterbottle was slung on the right-hand side in the usual way, but two men per section carried chagals - porous canvas bags holding nearly a quart of water. Each man had Bren magazines in his basic pouches and 100 rounds of ammunition slung around his waist in canvas bandoliers. The total transport consisted of about eighty mules, each capable of shouldering 160 lb. None could be spared for small arms, and Brens and 2-inch mortars had to be carried by the men. Four 3-inch mortar detachments with seventy-two bombs per mortar accompanied the Battalion and required most of the mules for their transport. Although there were six trained mortar detachments available, it seemed of little value to have more mortars but fewer bombs. The few mules left over carried reserve small arms ammunition, entrenching tools and water. One mule was allotted to the doctor for his stores. For the first operation, the adjutant and his orderly carried a couple of bottles of rum in their basic pouches as a contribution to the Officers' Mess. By a singular coincidence both broke their bottles, ostensibly owing to falls, while marching along hill paths at night. Thereafter one mule was detailed for the Battalion office. On one side its load consisted of such mundane articles as message pads, pencils and so on, balanced on the other by liquid refreshment for the British officers. The system worked well; the mule was teetotal, and the morale of the British officers was maintained.

In early April the 1st Indian Infantry Brigade was ordered to infiltrate across the lines of communication of the Japanese 15th Division and cut off a force that had captured the Litan saddle, an important feature on the approaches to Imphal. When the 1st Brigade was in position, the 37th, another brigade in the Division, was to attack the saddle frontally. Marching by night and lying up by day, it successfully accomplished the task and the Japanese were eliminated. But now came news that the headquarters of the 15th Division was at a village called Shongphel, only some eight map miles away - it was more nearly twenty by jungle trails over the Naga Hills. Orders came to liquidate this headquarters. The 1st/16th were to flush the Japanese out of the village, while other troops laid ambushes along the only possible paths for their retreat.

At 5 p.m. on 25 April the Battalion started out. It forded the Thoubal River and twelve hours later at 5 a.m. went into a hide a few miles short of Shongphel. Naga villagers interrogated by local guides - the village schoolmaster of Ukhrul rendered magnificent service both as guide and interpreter - talked gaily about 1,000-2,000 Japanese being quartered in Shongphel; the news was not passed on to the men, but Battalion Headquarters was a little silent and thoughtful that day. Next night the advance was resumed. About a mile short of Shongphel the track that the Battalion was following mounted a high ridge. Colonel Newell, assuming that the Japanese were certain to be holding the col where the track crossed this ridge, decided to turn off it well short of the crest. With the help of the splendid Naga guides the Battalion struck up the hillside through trackless jungle. Few who took part will ever forget the last three hours' climbing towards a skyline that forever receded. However, as the darkness began to lighten, the never-ending ascent, incredibly, came to an end. The ground no longer rose, instead it fell sharply away. In the pale light of dawn a village could be seen through the trees in the valley below. After a little discussion and compass work, it was confidently identified as Shongphel.

Colonel Newell now ordered 'B' Company to dig in on the ridge to form a firm base in the event of trouble, while the rest of the Battalion led by 'C' Company pressed along it to the col. 'C' Company advanced with its leading platoon deployed with all automatic weapons forward. For a short time the advance was wary and slow; then the platoon encountered some Japanese digging in. The automatics roared into action and a blast of fire smote the surprised Japanese; they fled, with 'C' Company in hot pursuit. The slow walk forward suddenly became a run that carried 'C' Company right across the col and up the slope the far side. The Japanese disappeared down a track that appeared to lead to the village, leaving a medium machine-gun behind them, and Colonel Newell took the opportunity to stop the headlong rush forward and impose some form of control. 'C' Company was ordered to take up a position on the far side of the col. 'D' Company was then to establish itself halfway down the track to Shongphel, after which 'A' Company was to pass through and penetrate into the village itself. Tactical Battalion Headquarters, the small operational component restricted to a few signallers and intelligence men needed for the minute-to-minute control of the Battalion, was to move with 'D' Company.

At noon 'D' Company started descending the track and took up a defensive position on a spur halfway down it; there was no sign of the Japanese. 'A' Company passed through, and soon bursts of fire announced that it had encountered opposition. With great verve, however, it pressed on. Then, dramatically, heavy fire broke out on the ridge where 'C' Company had taken up its position. Some Japanese had climbed on to the ridge beyond the company and were trying to drive on down to the col. The Battalion had a gunner officer with it, but unfortunately it had not proved possible to haul the guns within range; no assistance from outside could be expected. From 'C' Company came the news that their leading platoon was having difficulty in holding their hastily dug trenches. The situation began to look dangerous. If 'C' Company gave way, the 1st/16th would be irretrievably split. By now 'A' Company had entered the village itself, but the company commander had been wounded at its approaches. The news from 'C' Company became increasingly alarming. 'A' Company had accomplished their task and seized Shongphel; it appeared high time to concentrate the Battalion back on the ridge while 'C' Company still held out. This conclusion was reinforced when a Japanese light machine-gun opened up on 'D' Company. 'A' Company was called back and returned in excellent order, bringing with them a British 3-inch mortar and some Japanese discharger cups which they had captured in Shongphel; the sepoys had seen the back of the Japanese and were exultant.

As soon as 'A' Company was established across the col, 'D' Company retired through it and went on down the ridge to join 'B' Now came the delicate task of extricating 'C' Company. The men thinned out to re-form within the 'A' Company defences. Then the 3-inch mortars with pin-point accuracy dropped ten bombs by the forward weapons pits of 'C' Company and the last platoon of that company broke clear. The whole battalion now concentrated for the night on the position that 'B' Company had been constructing. All were alert for a night attack, but the hours of darkness passed quietly. Next day patrols pushed forward; they found no live Japanese, only a few corpses round the empty 'C' Company trenches beyond the col. That day the Battalion rested and in the evening Brigade Headquarters sent their congratulations together with the suggestion that Shongphel should be occupied. Some Japanese, withdrawing the previous night, had been ambushed, but other troops had been late into position and the jaws of the trap had failed to close. It was reported that headquarters of the Japanese Division had gone off the air. However that might be, one thing became clear: there were no Japanese in Shongphel,

On 30 April the Brigade was withdrawn into reserve at Wang Jing; it had not suffered many casualties and morale was extremely high. But a month of uncooked meals was beginning to tell, and lice had begun to appear on men's clothing; a change of raiment was somewhat overdue. Early in May the Battalion embarked on its toughest action of the battle. For some time now, the troops surrounded on the Imphal plateau had been entirely dependent on air supply; the two airstrips, one at Imphal, the other at Palel, were vital to the British and their capture was therefore the chief objective of the Japanese.

Toward Palel the main Japanese thrust had been along the Tamu-Palel road, but at the heights of Shenam which commanded that route they had been blocked after bitter fighting. They were now infiltrating north of the road and their artillery had begun to shell the Palel airstrip from positions underneath a mountain about 5,200 feet high which had been code-named ' Ben Nevis On 11 May the Battalion took to the hills with the aim of capturing Ben Nevis and forcing the Japanese to withdraw their guns. On the 12th, while they were proceeding down the track from Maibi Khunou towards Khudei Khunou, the Brigadier was encountered standing by the side of the path; he told Colonel Newell that a patrol of the Patiala Infantry, a company strong, had run into some Japanese on the ridge near Khudei Khunou and that he had ordered the Patialas to drive them out. As in the clear sunlight of a perfect morning the Battalion drew near the village, there came the sounds of heavy firing; a little farther on stretcher-bearers appeared carrying back Patiala casualties, always an enlivening spectacle before an engagement. The Battalion halted, while the Colonel walked forward to see the Patiala company commander. The latter reported he could not get on. The Japanese were entrenched on a crest overlooking the ridge which at this point was only about twenty yards wide with both sides falling away steeply into valleys some 500 feet below. They had heavy machine-guns covering the ridge approach and he thought they probably numbered a company. At this moment the Brigadier came up on the air; the 1st/16th were to attack the position and clear the Japanese out forthwith. A troop of a field battery, four guns, would give support; the gunners were limited to firing eighty shells, but, it was generously added, they were prepared to fire them any way that Colonel Newell wanted.

A straightforward attack down the ridge would certainly be costly and would most probably fail. The Colonel decided to send two companies down into the valley on a wide outflanking movement to come in on the Japanese from their flank and rear. While this move was in progress the gunners were to bombard the crest with a very slow rate of fire to be followed by a feint attack straight along it to keep the attention of the Japanese focused on the ridge. At about 3 p.m. 'A' and 'C' Companies started to descend into the valley; to avoid disclosing their movement from the inevitable noises of switched-on radio sets, they preserved wireless silence. The two companies disappeared into the jungle down the hillside and for three hours were neither heard nor seen. Then, as the daylight was going, a cascade of fire revealed that they had struck home. The roar of musketry, punctuated by the deep thud of grenades and the slow stutter of the Japanese heavy machine-guns, was moving unmistakably up the hill, to the jubilation of the watchers at Battalion Headquarters. Through the gathering darkness came the high-pitched 'Yah Ali' of the P.M.s followed by the deep baying 'Sat sri Akhal' of the Sikhs. The sound of battle reached the crest, then slowly faded and died. Over the radio came the voice of the 'C' Company commander. Khudei Khunou had been captured.

The attack had achieved complete surprise, falling upon the Japanese from a route so difficult that they had scarcely bothered to guard against it. The Battalion rested next day and patrolled forward. Except for some corpses there was no trace of the Japanese. The advance was resumed. Ahead, black and menacing, loomed the mighty bulk of Ben Nevis; that night the Battalion halted above the little village of Phalbung, some two miles short of the mountain destined to be its next objective. The slopes of Ben Nevis culminated in twin peaks about 400 yards apart. The ridge by Phalbung continued into the hillside about 500 yards below the right-hand peak. 'A' Company was pushed along the ridge just short of a knoll beyond which the ridge dipped into a shallow saddle before joining the slopes of the mountain itself. About 200 yards beyond the knoll the foremost bunker of the Jap position could be clearly discerned. Unusually for such skilled jungle fighters, although the bunker had been camouflaged with the branches of trees the camouflage had not been renewed, and the brown of the dead foliage stood out clearly against the green background. A good sign! Perhaps the Japanese were not from the redoubtable jungle division, the 33rd. For the next few days, although both sides could see each other, neither opened fire: the 1st/16th had no desire to alert their enemy; the Japanese thought perhaps that their position had not been observed.

The Battalion was once again on its own. The nearest unit of the Brigade, the Patiala Infantry, was between two and three miles away. It had to patrol widely to guard against surprise, but now, hardened as it was in jungle tactics, this caused little difficulty. The main target, however, was Ben Nevis. For a week, patrols combed the slopes of the mountain. Gradually a picture of the Jap dispositions emerged; they had entrenched two localities, one by each peak. The hillside was not precipitous, but steep and covered in high jungle, with here and there patches of dense undergrowth. Thanks to the jungle the two Jap positions were not inter-supporting; a daring patrol managed to penetrate between them and nearly reach the saddle between the two peaks. It was estimated that the Japanese amounted to about two infantry companies or a weak battalion.

Now Colonel Newell elaborated his plans. The attack would be supported by a complete regiment of artillery and a strike from the air. Even so, surprise would be vital. The Japanese obviously expected that an assault would come down the ridge from Phalbung, as this was far the easiest approach. Colonel Newell resolved not to use it, but to concentrate the Battalion in an assembly position in the valley and attack obliquely upwards. 'D' Company supported by 'A' would attack Left Peak; 'B' supported by 'D', Right Peak. Tactical Battalion Headquarters would be established on Knoll which afforded a limited view of the mountainside. The attack would be preceded by an air strike and artillery concentrations on both peaks. Brigade placed a company of Patiala Infantry under command to make a firm base on the ridge and be available to exploit a success.

On the evening of 23 May the companies moved out to their assembly areas and bedded down for the night. The air strike had been timed to go in at eight o'clock next morning. The dawn broke overcast and wet. The peaks were veiled in cloud. The air strike was postponed until ten o'clock while everyone studied the clouds anxiously watching for the first sign of a break. Suddenly the skies began to clear and, punctually at ten, flights of Vengeance dive-bombers roared into view. One by one the aircraft peeled off to come screaming down on the peaks. As their 500-lb. bombs exploded, great clouds of dust momentarily obscured the view; then the summits reappeared, to show tall trees tumbling to the ground. As the last of the bombers completed its mission the flights re-formed and sped away. Now Hurricane fighter-bombers came sweeping in to drop their lighter bombs on the Japanese and to strafe their positions with cannon and machine-gun fire. But suddenly things started to go wrong. Targets for the Vengeances had been indicated by artillery smoke and the smoke had drifted. The Hurricanes strafed and bombed short. Three came straight for Knoll, their guns blazing. Battalion Headquarters hugged the ground, but it was utterly unprotected. Earth spouted as bullets and cannon-shot slammed into the crest. Men fell crashing down the hillside. From the valley below came the dull boom of exploding bombs. An impassioned plea to Brigade Headquarters resulted eventually in the aircraft being called off, but Battalion Headquarters had suffered severely; among others, Colonel Newell had been seriously wounded and the Intelligence officer, also hit, had disappeared somewhere down the hillside. The rifle companies had escaped more lightly; the bombs had fallen into clumps of bamboo and their effect had been smothered. Nevertheless, each company had suffered one or two casualties; when bombs meant to support an attack fall instead on the attackers, it does little to stimulate the enthusiasm of men already slightly tensed at the prospect of imminent combat.

Now the guns opened up. They were firing at long range, about 9,000 yards; it had proved impossible to tow them any nearer; the changeable climatic conditions affected the flight of the shells and many fell wide. As the second-in-command took over and ordered the rifle companies forward, the omens for the day were far from auspicious. 'D' Company, attacking Left Peak, soon ran into trouble; attack after attack was shattered by the withering fire of the Japanese from well-concealed positions. The number of casualties mounted, while progress seemed impossible.

On the right the men of 'B' Company led. Their line of advance brought them obliquely against the Japanese trenches; they skirted them skilfully and through dense jungle forced their way to the top. The Jap position had been constructed on the forward slope well below the summit, probably as a precaution against strikes from the air. Now 'B' Company attacked downhill on their rear.

Unprepared for an assault from this direction, the Japs panicked and ran out towards Tengnoupal. At once 'B' and 'C' Companies dug in on Right Peak, pushing forward observation posts to give early warning of a counter-attack.

The situation now appeared to be that, while the attack on Left Peak had failed, Right Peak was firmly held. It was an invaluable characteristic of the operation that the regimental signallers never lost contact between headquarters and the rifle companies. Acting on the axiom of reinforcing success rather than failure, the second-in-command ordered the reserve company of Patialas forward to Right Peak, and accompanied them himself. He decided to use the Patiala company to attack Left Peak and called for an artillery concentration on that target. Although it had previously been registered, this was no easy task; shells ranged fractionally too far would spend themselves harmlessly in the valley beyond, while any short would pitch into 'D' Company just below the Japanese. Almost every shell had to be individually observed and observation itself was difficult. However, at about 4.30 p.m. the Patiala company commander, somewhat to his surprise, was told that the concentration had been fired and he left for Left Peak. The Patialas were highly trained and experienced soldiers. They took their time, nearly forty-five minutes, to cover 400 yards, but they also took Left Peak. Here again the main Japanese position had been dug below the crest. Now they were sandwiched with the Patialas above them and 'D' and 'A' Companies beneath. The second-in-command went to Left Peak to organize the final phase. A patrol was sent down to establish physical contact with the companies below; then 'A' Company launched a last desperate assault. For a few moments the fire was intense and a heavy blast struck the Patiala company. It was only to cover the Japanese withdrawal. 'A' Company surged up to Left Peak and began to dig in beside the Patialas. 'D' Company, a third of its strength wounded or dead, remained where it was. By nightfall all objectives had been captured.

Next day patrols revealed that the Japanese were gone, and now plans were made to replace the somewhat ad hoc defences of the previous evening. Right Peak was clearly the key to the position. This was made a double-company locality and here Battalion Headquarters was sited. Left Peak was held by another company and the fourth held Knoll on the Phalbung ridge. The position resembled a right-angled triangle with Right Peak at the right angle. During the day 'D' Company marched in, and the Patialas, their task completed, returned to their parent battalion.

The view from Ben Nevis was superb. The curves of the Tamu road were exposed to view, almost as far as the Lokchao River. While Ben Nevis was in British hands, a major offensive by the Japanese on the Shenam Heights was virtually impossible. Clearly the Japs would regard its recapture as a high priority. The Battalion prepared to hold what it had won. Trees were cut down and the timber used to build head cover over weapon pits. The localities were surrounded with bamboo fences, and punjis, sharpened bamboo stakes about eighteen inches long, were driven in along their base. The fences were also booby-trapped; for this purpose Mills hand-grenades, with the firing pin withdrawn, were placed in milk tins, and trip wires made from the strands of telephone cables were attached to the firing-levers. A fence was an excellent place for booby-traps: these dangerous little devices could backfire on their makers if their positions were not exactly recorded, but in a fence there was no danger of the wrong people being injured. No defence stores of any kind were available, of course; everything had to be improvised.

The Battalion enjoyed two days of tranquillity, presumably while the Japanese mustered their forces. It may seem strange that the British forces at Shenam could do nothing to pin down the troops on their front. The task of the 23rd Division at this time was essentially defensive. While Imphal was beleaguered, resources in fire-power had to be carefully husbanded. Of necessity, the main effort had to be directed to reopening the road to Kohima and re-establishing ground communications with India. The role of the 23rd Division was to hold the Palel airstrip and for this the possession of the Shenam Heights was vital. If the Japanese had to withdraw resources from before Shenam this suited the divisional plan, however much the 1st/16th might deplore it.

So the Battalion strengthened its defences and awaited the inevitable. On the third day it happened. During the late afternoon Japanese 105 and 155 mm. guns started to bombard the peaks. Against the heavy 155 mm. shells the head cover on the weapon pits offered little protection. Many shells struck the trees and burst in the air, their fragments scything down on what lay below. For some reason the brunt of the bombardment fell on Left Peak and here 'A' Company suffered severely. Then, in the small hours of the morning, screaming Japanese infantry came charging through the darkness. They were surprised by the strength of Right Peak and before the steady fire of the defenders found themselves unable to make any impression. At daybreak, baffled, they dug in about 100 yards below the Right Peak perimeter.

Next morning 'A' Company was moved from Left Peak to the comparative safety of Knoll. Knoll, under the shadow of Ben Nevis, was immune to shellfire from the far side of that mountain. For the next ten days a recurrent pattern set in. By day the Japanese sporadically shelled the mountain top;

anything they could see moving, they sniped with 75 mm. field guns emplaced nearby. By night their infantry attacked, normally after the moon was down. Only the night of the full moon was quiet. Night after night they were foiled by the fire from the perimeter, the pounding of the 25-pounders sited in the distant Sengmai Turel and the devastating accuracy of the 3-inch mortars. Two had been sited in Right Peak and one in each of the other localities to cover ground which, owing to the steepness of the hillside, could not be reached by the guns. The mortars fired at a range of 100 yards, well inside their authorized minimum. Each night they re-registered their targets by the simple method of screwing their mortars upwards until the bombs descended on the forward trenches; their occupants considered that, since they were protected and the Japs in the open, the risk was worth taking.

As night after night they fired on their defensive targets, complaints came up from the gun lines that the gunners were getting no rest; the news was received without sympathy. On the mountain, after the first bombardment, all the mules had been evacuated. Water had to be carried up by hand from a spring 300 feet below. By day the men removed their boots for a couple of hours to prevent their feet becoming soft; there could be no question of taking them off at night. As time passed the men became lousy, and after more than a month on the American 'K' ration, during which no form of cooked meal had been eaten, their physical condition began to deteriorate. Slowly, from shellfire and sickness, the Battalion's strength drained away. A draft of ninety men joined on the mountain - what a place to join a unit, the adjutant reflected - but this soon dwindled away. Every night the trenches were manned, every night the attacks were repelled. The Japanese could not always retrieve their dead, and the sickly smell of decaying corpses was added to the other pleasures of the mountain resort.

As the strength of the Battalion ebbed away, it became apparent that the time would come when the trenches could not be properly manned, and that one night the Battalion would be overrun. The Divisional Commander had been watching the situation and now concluded that Ben Nevis was too exposed and the problems of supply too great to justify continuing to hold the mountain. The operation had fulfilled its purpose. For a fortnight it had diverted the main Japanese thrust away from the Palel road; now he resolved not to relieve the 1st/16th but to evacuate.

Ironically, while the orders for the evacuation were going out on 6 June, the Japanese launched their heaviest bombardment. By now they had pinpointed every inch of the position and they proceeded to search it yard by yard. They had recognized the importance of Right Peak and directed almost the whole of their fire on it. Two miles away Brigade Headquarters, aghast, watched a flaming torrent of shells exploding on the mountain top. It seemed to them incredible that anyone could live underneath such a bombardment. Somehow the word got about that the Battalion had withdrawn.

The order went to the guns in the Sengmai Turel to fire ten rounds gunfire into the Right Peak. At this time all the gunner communications on Ben Nevis had been destroyed; the gunner signaller lay dead, with his officer lying mortally wounded across his body. But fortunately the brigade radio set was still in order, and the adjutant contrived a pungent conversation with the Brigade Major. He afterwards swore that a piece of molten metal whizzed between his lips and the mouthpiece of the radio.

Then, as always, with the coming of darkness the Japanese guns fell silent and it was possible to take stock. Right Peak was almost unrecognizable. Twisted tree-trunks lay strewn across the ground, and a great pit yawned where presumably a number of shells had fallen together. 'D' Company held the front face of the position and had been savagely mauled. Company Head-quarters had been hit and the company commander wounded; the Japanese had blasted the forward bunkers with a 75 mm field gun at a range of 500 yards and had blown away half the forward platoon. The sole surviving

V.C.O. took over. Reinforcements were called for from Knoll; the battery commander, who had survived by a miracle, worked frantically to restore communications with the guns. By evening stand-to some sort of order had been imposed. Had the Japanese attacked immediately after the shelling, the Battalion must have been overrun, but they waited for nightfall, and that gave the 1st/16th a chance.

As the darkness deepened the Battalion waited grimly for the events of the night to unfold. It rather resembled the outer rind of a cheese from which the cheese itself had been removed: every man, batman, cook, orderly, clerk, was manning the outer trenches; inside there was nothing save the two mortar detachments and the brigade signal terminal. At ten the Japs came. Their leading ranks started to break through the bamboo face thirty yards away from the trenches, and for a few crucial moments the hard-tried men of 'D' Company wavered. Then came the order for rapid fire; the mortars opened up and far away in the Sengmai Turel a distant sound like the beating of a heavy drum told that the guns were once more in action. The line held; against so fierce a fire the Japanese had no hope. They returned to the attack again at two in the morning, but they had no stomach for a fight which they knew to be hopeless; they faded away as the first automatics opened up from the perimeter.

For the rest of the night the silence was intense. Then with the dawn came the rain. Fortune was favouring the 1st/ 16th. As the heavy clouds closed down, not a sound was to be heard from the Japanese lines. At nine o'clock a host of stretcher-bearers arrived from Brigade Headquarters. It was a ten-mile carry over rough hill-tracks to road-head; a badly wounded man had little hope. Then the mules came, were loaded up and were gone. The grey clouds hung around the mountain face and masked the Battalion as it quietly filtered away. By 2 p.m. Ben Nevis was clear. Not a shot had been fired. Except for 'A' Company remaining on Knoll to cover the withdrawal, the remainder of the Battalion marched back to the gun lines in the Sengmai Turel. That night the gunners, whose unstinting assistance had contributed so much to the successful defence, insisted on taking over the night guards to give the Battalion an uninterrupted sleep. It was a generous gesture and much appreciated, although it was probably several days before the reflex reactions after the past fortnight permitted unbroken slumber.

Next day 'A' Company re-joined. The company commander reported that during the night they had heard the Japanese firing on the trenches of Ben Nevis; they had called down fire to keep them amused, but towards morning a shout of triumph had indicated that the Japs had found the trenches empty.

The Battalion, sick, weary, lousy, was withdrawn into Corps reserve. All its clothing had to be destroyed; for six weeks the men had neither washed nor eaten cooked food, and the first taste of normal cooked meals on stomachs unused to any type of fat or grease was certain to provoke an upset. During the first week 150 men went sick. But they soon recovered and spirits rose high. All felt that the reverse in the Chin Hills had now been avenged. During the fighting round Ben Nevis, the strength of the Battalion rarely exceeded 450, since all drivers, members of the carrier platoon, two mortar detachments and various duty men, had to be left at base. It suffered 153 casualties; apart from those inflicted during the initial assault, almost all the remainder could be attributed to shellfire.

From A History of the Goth Punjabis by Lt Col J. P. Lawford (Osprey Publishing Ltd, 1972)

The SAS, or - to give it its full title - the Special Air Service Regiment, was one of the most remarkable creations of the Second World War. Like the Commandos it was meant to produce fear and destruction in enemy ranks but whereas the Commandos would approach by sea the SAS originally intended to approach by parachute.

The SAS was formed in ig4i by David Stirling, then a second lieutenant in the Scots Guards. He reasoned that as most German aircraft were too fast and manoeuvrable to be destroyed in the air they must be destroyed on the ground on their own airfields. Stirling and his friends obtained permission and an unsuitable aircraft with which to teach themselves parachuting; not surprisingly the experience was not without accidents. Eventually it was discovered that the best means of reaching airfields in the Middle East was by crossing the desert in trucks or jeeps and walking the last ten or twenty miles. Subsequently they destroyed 350 planes, huge quantities of stores, rail tracks, etc., and caused the wholesale diversion of large numbers of German troops from their intended activities. Later they continued their activities in Sicily, Italy, the Greek islands, France and Germany, In France they remained for long periods behind the enemy lines.

At the end of the war the SAS was disbanded but it was re-formed to fight Communist terrorists in the depths of the Malayan jungle. Here, and later in Borneo, they adapted themselves to living in houses or holes, in swamps or camps. Although all SAS soldiers are parachutists most of them are also skilled mountaineers, drivers, canoeists, and skiers. However, in the final analysis the SAS consider that legs are probably the most reliable form of transport.

The first passage here is a description of the early days of raiding airfields in the Second World War; the second is of tracking terrorists in the Malayan jungle. The reader may feel that they illustrate a considerable difference of terrain and technique.

Getting on to the airfield was not easy, as it was wired and guarded. Fortunately for the SAS an RAF plane chose that moment to drop a stick of bombs across the runway, and in the resultant confusion the SAS party planted bombs on twenty-one planes and a number of other targets. They slipped away from the airfield without casualties and later in the night were able to look back and see their bombs exploding. Another twenty-four hours took them to within a few miles of the beach, where they concealed themselves until they could be taken off. Jellicoe and their one Greek guide - Lieutenant Costi - went off to a nearby village to make contact with a Cretan who would signal to the submarine. Unfortunately, in the meantime, the party's hiding place had been accidentally discovered by a party of Cretans and betrayed to the Germans. The result was that Berge suddenly found himself the objective of three separate German patrols. Although he decided to fight in the hope that he might escape after dark, the party, already heavily outnumbered, had only Tommy guns which soon ran out of ammunition. All were killed or captured. When Jellicoe returned with the information about the rendezvous for being taken off he could find no trace of Berge's party. He soon enquired from nearby peasants what had happened and learnt that Berge and the other prisoners had been taken to Heraklion. Jellicoe embarked three days later with twenty refugees. It had been a disaster, but it had also been a victory, for the Crete expedition had destroyed more than the other two parties combined.

In spite of the raids, the Malta convoy took a tremendous hammering, losing fifteen out of seventeen ships; nevertheless the two ships which did get through carried enough supplies to tide Malta over till the next convoy, or part of it, arrived. Whether the thirty-seven aircraft which the SAS destroyed in their raids that night might have sunk the remaining two ships is anyone's guess but there was no doubt in the minds of the German command that this steadily increasing destruction of valuable aircraft was dangerous as well as humiliating and must be stopped at the earliest possible moment.

Meanwhile, in every other way, the campaign was going superbly for the Germans. Tobruk, with its vast supplies, surrendered to them, and the whole of the British army was falling back towards Alamein. German troops had already crossed the Egyptian frontier and although their advance was not without loss it seemed to many as if their next stop would be Cairo. There was considerable alarm in what had been thought to be secure rear areas; documents were burnt and all the morale-destroying programme of evacuation was in full swing. But morale, in some people, is an unpredictable and effervescent substance. This dramatic change in the military situation presented the SAS with an emergency role for which it was not entirely suited, but also gave to Stirling the opportunity to acquire vehicles and armaments which were ideal under any conditions. These were 'jeeps', the small American GPs - general purpose trucks - which were fast, mobile, manoeuvrable, inconspicuous and uncomfortable; and Vickers K guns. Vickers Ks were aircraft guns which had formerly been mounted in the Gloster Gladiator fighter aircraft. As this plane was now obsolete the RAF had spare supplies of Vickers in their workshops and Stirling, who had come across them by accident, laid his hands on all he could acquire. They were mounted in pairs at the front and rear of the jeeps, and later supplemented with a .50 Browning. The Vickers could be electronically controlled, but whether used singly or in pairs their effect was devastating. An average rate of fire was 1,200 rounds a minute, and the noise was so shattering that it virtually contributed to the firepower. A truck caught by a Vickers K would disintegrate. Occasionally the Vickers jammed, but meticulous maintenance reduced such hazards to the minimum.

The whole of the SAS became mobile. All the supplies which could possibly be taken were loaded on to three-tonners, twenty in number. By this means their programme could be more flexible; and they could stay in the desert for approximately three weeks, barring accidents. All that remained was to obtain a full report of the general situation, be briefed on the most desirable targets, and go. However, there were accidents. The sand was too soft for the heavily laden lorries and, after numerous delays, many of the supplies were abandoned and the party reduced drastically in numbers. The remainder drove on; it was not clear where they would find a hole in the enemy lines but they would find out by looking. And they found it. Navigated by Gurdon of the LRDG* they travelled 150 miles without encountering enemy opposition and then linked up with another LRDG party under Timpson, also of the LRDG. These two highly capable and experienced LRDG officers would then be available to pilot the SAS parties to whatever targets were thought suitable.

* Long Range Desert Group, an independent unit which patrolled vast areas of desert to obtain information about enemy movements and strength.

On this occasion the raiding plan was based on the somewhat optimistic assumption that the British army, having retreated this far, would now turn and take the offensive. In the event the offensive proved abortive but the SAS gained some useful experience. Mayne was given the task of destroying planes on the Bagush airfield while Stirling established a road block and ambush on what had been predicted as being an important enemy supply route. The traffic failed to materialise, but Mayne succeeded in reaching the airfield and planting bombs on forty aircraft. Much to his irritation half the bombs failed to explode, having become damp, and it seemed that some eighteen aircraft would have to be left intact on the airfield. At this point Stirling decided to see what the new Vickers Ks could do. He and Mayne drove around the perimeter of the airfield and shot seven aircraft to pieces. Clearly the new guns could do as much, and more, than had been expected. The other parties had had varied fortune, chiefly because the airfields they raided were now being much more carefully guarded. Even so, the bag amounted to some seventeen aircraft and a large number of trucks. The return journey was hazardous but the only casualties were to their transport. By this time the SAS were highly experienced in dodging enemy aircraft or - if destruction was imminent - abandoning the vehicle and making a run for it.

As soon as they had taken stock the SAS were off again, this time in five parties. They had varying fortunes. Mayne's was the most successful, destroying fifteen aircraft; a good part of Mayne's 'luck' was probably due to quicker thinking and greater experience, but some people do seem to be luckier than others and they make good commanders. The greatest loss on this expedition was that of Gurdon, who had been killed by enemy aircraft - which he was trying to shoot down. Although not a member of the SAS - he was just about to transfer to them - he had, as a member of the LRDG, made a tremendous contribution to its successes.

By this time it was necessary to obtain more supplies; both food and ammunition were running low. A resupply party consisting of three jeeps and eight trucks was organised and included Lieutenant Scratchley, well known to the peacetime world as a steeplechaser. In the event it turned out to be his roughest ride ever.

By now the Germans had established themselves in the areas through which the SAS had previously passed without difficulty; it was therefore necessary to go back through the Qattarra Depression which had one track of doubtful firmness across it; the remainder was salt bog with a thin crust which would not bear the weight of a vehicle.

The crossing was made by day, which meant that the heat haze concealed the party from patrolling aircraft, but they were exposed to intense heat of the most unpleasant kind. Owing to the roughness and uncertainty of the track, progress was slow - a few miles an hour - and periodically the convoy had to stop to change a tyre. Conditions such as these would have been in-supportable for men less fit and experienced, and without high morale. This was the sort of situation where moral courage takes over from physical and raises the limit of endurance. Less torrid conditions have produced heatstroke and mental disorder among men who, although sound enough, simply had not the requisite experience and morale. As an example of the latter one of the trucks was set alight by an enemy air attack early on the trip. While it was burning three men removed the wheels because, as they put it, 'the tyres might come in useful'.

Within eight days the resupply party had returned with twenty jeeps, Vickers Ks and stores of all varieties. With this new equipment it was planned to make a straightforward attack on Sidi-Enich airfield, which was reputed to be crammed with aircraft of every variety. On this occasion it was decided that a different technique was needed. The Germans were not submitting tamely to the destruction of their planes and had adopted every measure possible which did not involve the large scale use of troops. They had begun by making a man sleep beneath the wing of every plane. When this proved unsatisfactory the perimeter was more carefully guarded, searchlights were mounted, and armoured cars were attached to some of the larger fields. The new method the SAS would therefore employ would be to arrive with such firepower that the defences would be overwhelmed.

Stirling planned the raid like a drill movement. The three leading jeeps would clear the route ahead as the party moved down the runway and the other jeeps would give their attention to the planes parked alongside. The raid was carefully practised in darkness. With the jeeps five yards apart it was important that formation should be strictly maintained, otherwise some of the bullets would find the wrong targets. Navigation was in the hands of Sadler who was meticulously accurate in spite of rough going and obstacles. They arrived at the airfield on time.

To their surprise the airfield was not in darkness as they expected but brilliantly lit. The runways were in full use, with planes landing and taking off. Into the well-organised scene suddenly appeared a force of eighteen jeeps, all but one of which were positioned to use their four Vickers K guns.

Consequently the firepower of this little convoy amounted to some 68 guns, each capable of firing 1,200 rounds a minute. As it moved down the middle of the airfield it created a scene which almost defies description. Formation was rigidly maintained, and the sweep of destruction reaped a harvest beyond the most optimistic dream. In a few moments the crowded airfield was so full of blazing and exploding planes that the SAS men had their hair singed and faces scorched. The Germans were caught completely by surprise - one plane was destroyed as it landed - but a mortar and a Breda soon began a steady but not particularly effective response. Having gone through the middle of the airfield the jeep party paused, reformed and made a sweep around the perimeter. In the last round they added a number of Junkers 88s and some stores buildings to their total. It was a classic display of ingenuity, control, firepower, skill and surprise. Every plane on the airfield had been destroyed. It was the sort of demonstration which does enemy morale no good at all.

Wild animals were not as difficult as might be thought. Perhaps the most intense moment was that experienced by Sergeant Turnbull's patrol. They heard noises and took up ambush positions. Into the ambush walked a huge bull elephant, a little too large for the grenades they were holding with the pins out. The patrol scattered smartly and fortunately the elephant also decided to change direction. Tigers, with which Malaya abounds, usually took evasive action although on several occasions a patrol met a tiger face to face. Only old tigers become man-eaters, but the SAS were in no position to guess a tiger's age when they turned a comer and met one; usually the tiger disappeared before it could be questioned. Most dangerous of all animals was the seladang - or water buffalo - for it would circle and then charge without warning.

Snakes were rather more of a problem because they were plentiful and live in the sort of places which one might use for hasty concealment, as would scorpions. A snake will usually move swiftly away, but occasionally one would decide on a confrontation and had to be shot. The krait was particularly deadly and would sometimes rear up in the middle of a track.

Leeches were a frequent problem and there was no apparent answer to them. A big leech such as a lanchen could take half a pint of blood before being detected and removed. One man was seen to have 74 small leeches around his ankles. Removing them was difficult and required salt or a lighted cigarette. Leeches had extraordinary penetrative powers and could get in through the eyelet in a boot. They would come not only from damp ground but also from tree branches. If a patrol was in an area infested with leeches it was philosophically accepted that some - perhaps many - would get on to them. They were painless and therefore would not be detected for a while, although they might become painful later. The leech clearly had some anti-coagulant in its mouth for the bites would ooze blood for some fifteen minutes after its removal. Woodhouse's* first experience of leeches was when he stripped down one night and found seventeen inside his trouser waistband; the blood ran to his ankles as he removed them. Fortunately leeches were not encountered in swamps, except when they dropped off trees. The worst area for leeches was the Kerbau valley, where they advanced towards the intruder like jerky little inverted Vs. Fortunately it was possible to avoid them at night for they would not venture on to a dry surface such as a poncho.

Lt Col J. M. Woodhouse was with the SAS in the jungle and was generally reckoned as a leader of outstanding quality. Later he commanded the unit.

The two most dangerous insects were hornets and mosquitoes. Hornets, which were of the thickness of the forefinger, had a powerful sting and were easily disturbed; mosquitoes were everywhere and, of course, apart from the irritation of their bites, carried malaria.

There were a host of minor irritations such as ants and ticks, and skin infections which are inevitable in a hot, wet, climate. Prickly heat - a rash which can irritate until a man wishes to tear the skin off his body — tineas of various descriptions, such as footrot, were almost too familiar to deserve comment. The SAS were wryly amused when a police officer's wife was horrified to see aborigine women wearing nothing but a loincloth. She hastily provided them with bras - and in consequence tinea. Although the SAS were by no means immune to the charm of women when on leave, aborigine women were sacrosanct. Major Dare Newell had laid down: 'When dealing with guerillas ignore their women folk like poison; the women might not appreciate it but the men will.'

'Jungle' covered a wide variety of conditions. There was forest which consisted of large trees up to 200 feet high with their branches interlaced at the top, and there was bamboo which grew in clumps and fell in all directions, some of it being full of spiky thorns. Bamboo could be one of the most difficult types of jungle. Then there would be Lalang, tall grass up to 12 feet high, probably rich in snakes. This would reflect the sun and be extremely hot. And of course there was thick scrub where everything had grown into a tangled mass.

The governing features of Malaya were a high temperature, high rainfall, and high humidity. This meant that vegetables grew with great speed; you can plant a pumpkin seed and ten weeks later eat the pumpkin which has grown from it. The country, including the mountainous area, is therefore covered with a thick coating of vegetation and under that cover the land may be reasonably dry or may be swamp. Swamp is not, of course, all of one type but in general is about thigh deep. Some swamp is caused by heavy rainfall and dries out in the dry season, other swamp is permanent. The water is full of trees and their entwined roots, mud and leaves. It is usually reddish, like the soil. Passage through swamps was by wading and was; inevitably slow; sometimes it entailed clambering over tree roots or hacking through tangled branches.

In the spring of 1958 an extraordinary operation took place near Telok Anson, about 30 miles north-west of Kuala Lumpur in a swamp measuring approximately 10 by 18 miles. D Squadron under Major H. Thompson - who had been invalided home with chest trouble in 1955 but had recovered - knew there were Communist Terrorists living in the swamp and decided to winkle them out. The squadron had already considerable experience of living and operating in swamps. Their objective was two groups of CTs who had lived in the swamp many years under the leadership of Ah Hoi, nicknamed the 'Baby-killer'. They had a tremendous nuisance value over a very wide area and large numbers of troops had to be allocated to protective work because the CTs could not be tracked and eliminated. D Squadron parachuted in about 3 miles from the western edge, and gradually tracked the Communist Terrorists down. The squadron adapted itself to swamp life, and apparently found it pleasanter than many other areas they had been in. Not everyone would agree about swamp life being preferable to life elsewhere. Swamps in certain areas were up to twenty feet deep, extremely hot and infested with snakes. Men slept in hammocks, and got out every morning into water - in which they stayed all day. This, as they put it, was 1 less enjoyable than walking along the tops of mountain ridges, when with a little imagination you could think you were going for a Sunday afternoon stroll '. The swamp was warmer than the hills at night and the sickness rate was low. They attributed the fact that swamp life was comparatively healthy to the iron in the water. It could of course have been otherwise, for some water in Malaya, and elsewhere, is contaminated with leptospirosis, a germ passed in rats' urine which enters the body through scratches or drinking. Leptospirosis takes about ten days to develop and is usually fatal. The bigger trees grew on a cupola of roots and this enabled both the SAS and CTs to build secure and comfortable bashas between the buttresses. By digging down between these roots they could also obtain clear water. Such hideouts were particularly advantageous for the Communists for it was extremely difficult to approach through the water without making some noise.

It is not, unfortunately, possible to give a detailed account of this operation here, but it ended in the complete elimination of the terrorists from the area. A considerable factor in its success was the skill shown in tracking. It is well known that Ibans were imported from Borneo to assist in tracking but it is probably less well known that British soldiers also developed an extraordinary skill in this art - and in not leaving tracks themselves - in every area. In the swamps they could follow from a piece of dislodged bark, a twisted leaf and so on. Notable among British trackers was Sergeant Turnbull who was better than the Ibans and more consistent. Turnbull was a Yorkshireman who had joined the Royal Artillery 'in order to see a bit of the world'. He joined the SAS and showed an exceptional ability to learn. He learnt three things exceptionally quickly and well: one was the ability to shoot fast but under perfect control, the second was fluent Malay so that he could talk to aborigines and Ibans as if it was a first language, and, as mentioned, tracking. On this operation he tracked the Communists for some 14 weeks, including a ten-mile stretch in the last week. Tracking, whether in swamp or otherwise, is an exhausting activity because it requires constant, nonstop, concentrated observation, and, of course, can be frustrating. Turnbull missed nothing, and could move with the speed and agility of a cat. He carried a repeater shot gun — as many did and this would fill a man with holes like a Gruyere cheese.

On one occasion just when his patrol was moving off south-east of Legap they spotted a terrorist some 20 yards away. Major Cartwright, who was then a new subaltern, said that Turnbull fired with such speed that the first three shots made an almost continuous bang. By the time the echoes died away Turnbull was standing over the terrorist to make sure he did not need a fourth. The terrorist on this occasion was the famous Ah Tuck, an important Communist organiser who had a great influence on the aborigines. Other expert trackers were Sergeant McFarland, an ex-Seaforth Highlander, Sergeant Hawkins and Sergeant Creighton. Tracking in Malaya was complicated by the fact that rain might destroy traces and the terrorists, once alerted, would move very fast indeed, faster, in fact, than British troops.

By the end of 1958 a massive anti-terrorist organisation had been built up in Malaya, and the SAS were only a small part of it. Some 6,398 terrorists had been killed and another 3,000 had been captured or had surrendered. The terrorists seemed to attract a flow of recruits although many of these became bored by the indoctrination. However, once a terrorist, you would be unlikely to give up easily - you might be disposed of if you appeared to waver and therefore endangered the group. However, many surrendered and were induced to persuade others. On our side 3,000 civilians and 2,000 of the security forces had been killed. Planters had displayed remarkable courage throughout the entire emergency although many were killed. The biggest factor in causing CT surrenders were the loss of leaders and the cutting off of food supplies.

From A History of the Special Air Service by Philip Warner (Class Warfare 2014)

Maps

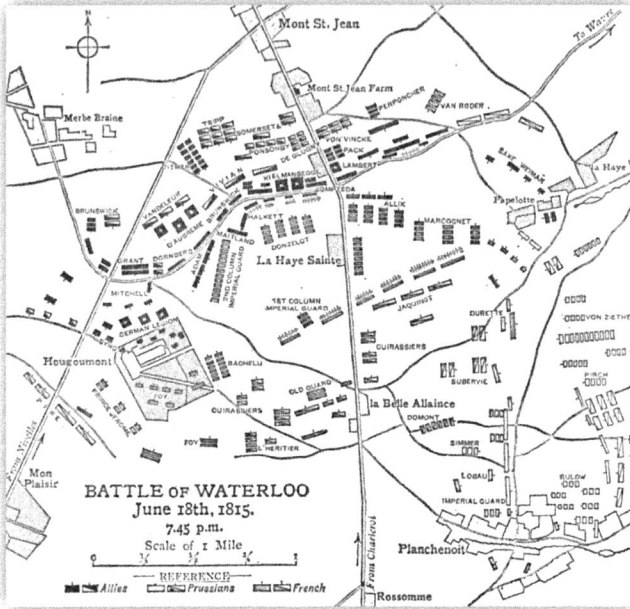

Battle of Waterloo, 18 June 1815 7.45pm

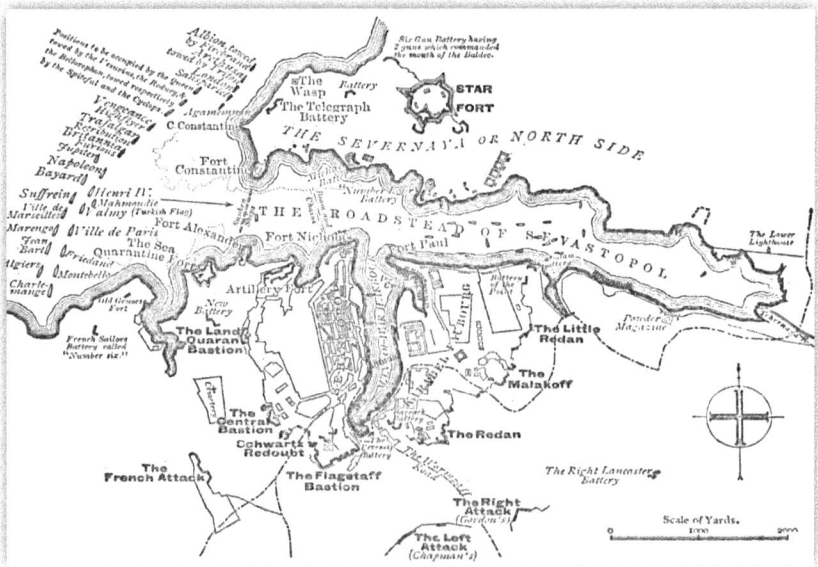

Plan of the siege of Sebastopol

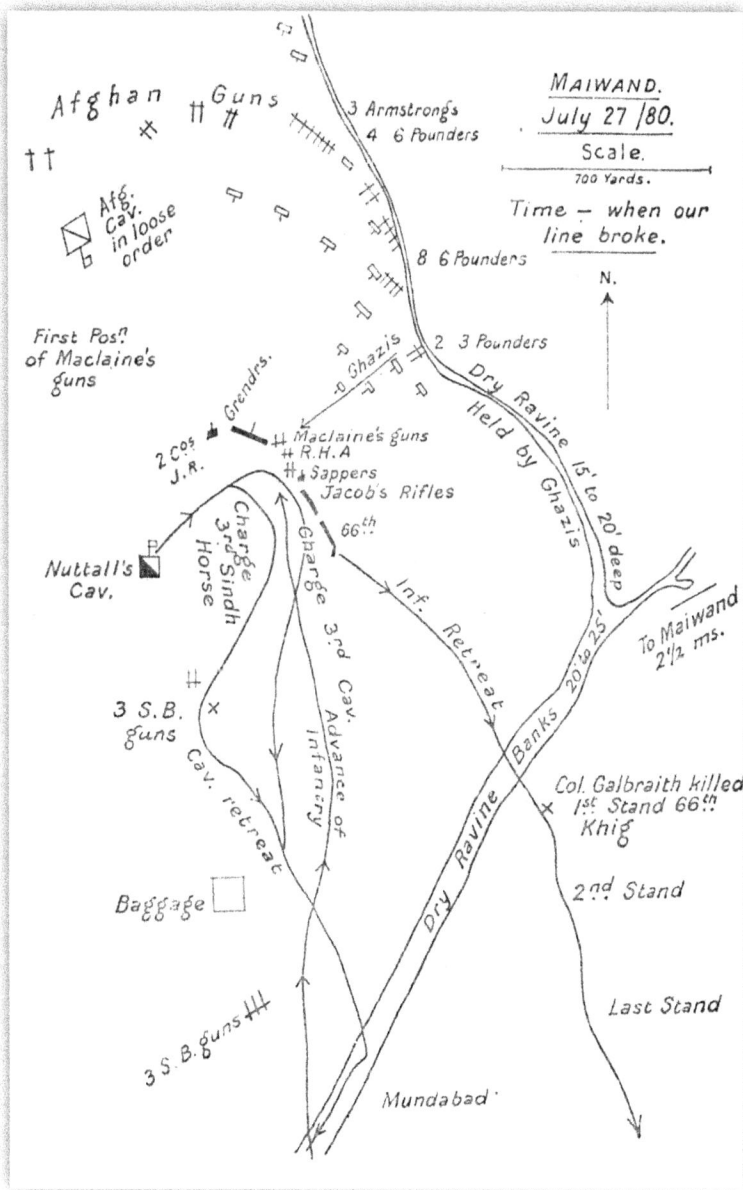

Maiwand, 27 July 1880

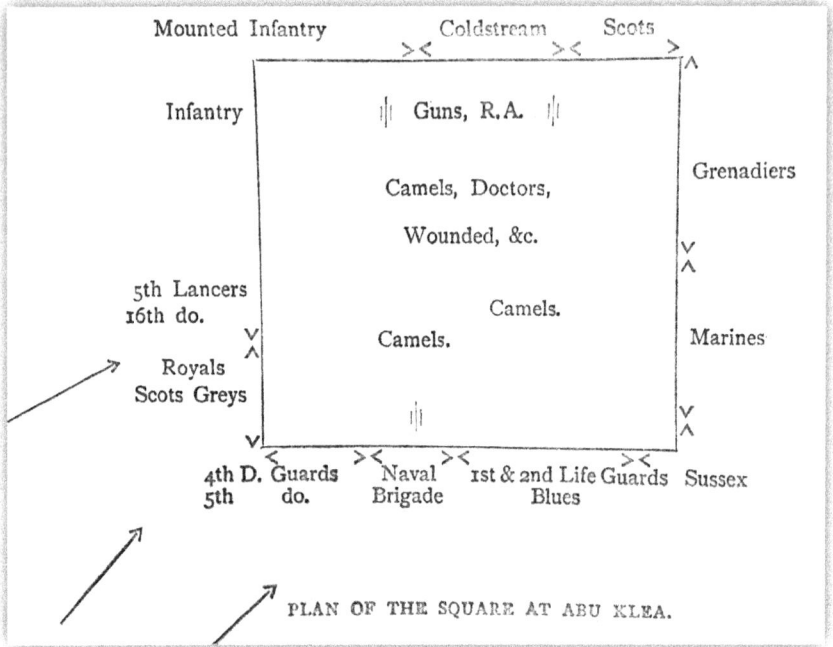

Plan of the Square at Abu Klea

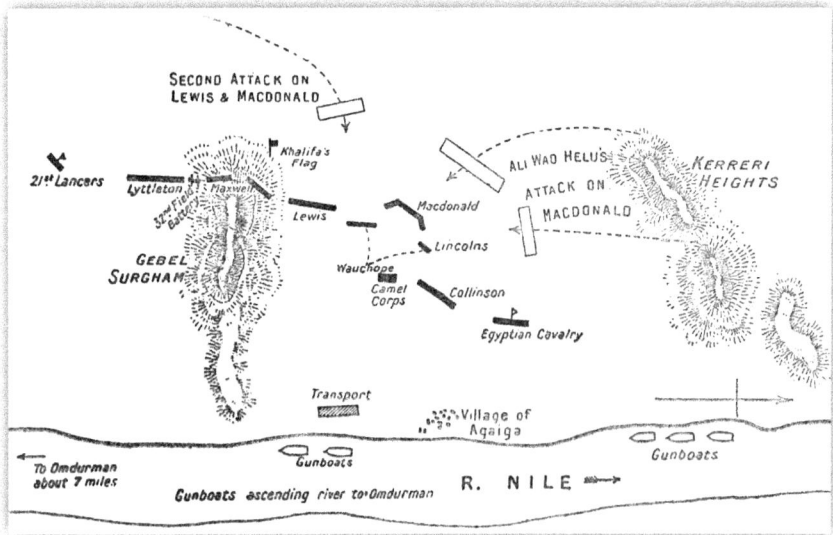

Battle of Omdurman, Phase Three, 10.10 am

The fall of the Duke of Brunswick at the Battle of Quatre Bras, 1811

The Fusiliers in action at the Battle of Albuera, 1811

The Battle of Vitoria, 1813

Early photograph of a gun emplacement at Balaclava showing the use of fascines in fortifications

The charge of the Heavy Brigade at Balaclava, 1854

The charge of the ill-fortuned Light Brigade, 1854

The Russians retreating from the south side of Sebastapol, 1855

A view of the interior of the Redan looking south towards the salient angle

The heroic stand of the last eleven at Maiwand, 1880

The dash with the colours at Isandhlwana, 1879

Sir Redvers Buller's retreat: the enemy pursuing and attacking at Abu Klea,1885

Officers and attached officers of the 21st Lancers who participated in the Battle of Omdurman, 1898

Victims of poison gas in the First World War

Men of the Punjab Regiment boarding a British troopship for India, their task of disarming the Japanese in southern Indo-China complete

Air rescue by the SAS regiment in the Malayan Jungle, 1953

Historians are like deaf people who go on answering questions that no one has asked them.
Leo Tolstoy

The true worth of an individual is valued in many ways but for an historian how can we know their worth? I think many would agree that it is an ability to ask and answer questions that many would shy away from. Tolstoy would certainly agree with that and one of the finest military historians England has produced in the 20th Century Philip Warner ably matches this description.

His style is engaging but absolutely honest. He will not sugar coat when the bitter facts need to be faced. He will make an allowance for the stresses and needs of war but he will explain them for what they are not for what the victor would rather they be.

Below is not a formal biography but a personal tribute given by his son, Richard Warner, at his funeral. It's a marvellous piece of explanation and devotion that illuminates the man and his work:

I rang the Book Review Editor of *The Spectator* last week to tell him that Philip had died and therefore please not to send more books to review. I introduced myself as 'Richard Warner, Philip Warner's son'. He replied 'that is a very nice thing to be able to say'.

He was absolutely right and it does feel very nice, doesn't it, to be a child of Philip's, or a member of

Philip's family, or one of Philip's much cherished friends and work colleagues, and indeed nice to have enjoyed Philip's stimulating company.

He prized above all the loyalty of family and those firm friends who he included inside that inner circle. Once you had won his trust and respect, then you were on his side and he would do anything for you. 'Families stick together through thick and thin'. You didn't let the side down. If one did, he would be slow to forgive and never to forget.

So, as his family and friends, I welcome you all here today to the Royal Memorial Chapel, to join in this Service of Thanksgiving for Philip.

Philip did not 'meekly hand in his dinner pail', as P. G. Wodehouse put it – he remained an active, alert, interested and interesting man right to the end.

He died just under a fortnight ago, aged 86, on September 23rd, peacefully in his sleep, beside his great love and companion for the last 30 years, Freda. He had gone to bed with a copy of *The Spectator*, in which he had written a review of a biography of a hero of his – Jock Lewes, co-founder of the Special Air Service. He had finished his day as he always did, reading a chapter from Wodehouse. He just did not wake up to make the early morning tea.

He was – in his words – 'going like a train' (an expression he had learned before the era of Connex South Central), enjoying a very busy life in his fourteenth year as the army obituarist on *The Daily Telegraph* (he had filed his last obit on the day before), a regular book reviewer for *The Spectator*, *The Field*, and many other papers and periodicals.

It is perhaps only in the last fortnight that the Warner family has come to realise what a special man our father was, and just how many facets there were to his life. Each of us has found out more about this reserved, steadfast, lively-minded and inspiring man from letters or telephone calls since his death.

He had special, private, individual friendships with a large number of you – but since he did not talk about himself, the facts of his life are not well known. When teaching us to box, he encouraged to 'present a moving target' – and he took this advice better than anyone. When his close friends and next door neighbours of some forty years found out only from his obituary in the *Telegraph* that he had been a Prisoner of War, let alone a guest of the Japanese, I realised we need to – in his words – 'establish some facts'.

Philip was born the youngest child of three and the only boy into a farming family in Warwickshire, deep in the countryside, on May 19th 1914, just four months before the First World War.

Philip proudly traced his ancestry back some 500 years in the same county, loving this continuity with the past that he picked out in his first book, published in 1968, *Sieges of The Middle Ages*:

'Standing on the battlements of a castle the humblest person feels a sense of power and grandeur. He is back in the past and feels a kinship with the original owners. In all probability this kinship is genuine, though remote. Every family that was in England in 1087 is now related thirteen times over to every other family in the country at that time; he is thus related both to the mighty baron and the most downtrodden villein.'

The Warner family sold their farm in 1924, which meant that Philip had to put up with poor local schooling, making him determined that his children would have the opportunity of public school education that he had missed – never mind whether he could afford it or not.

He strongly believed that 'nothing is impossible, you can do anything, if you put your mind to it – and persevere at it'. His achievement in winning a County Major Scholarship from Nuneaton Grammar School, against all expectations, to Christ Church, Oxford, was a prime example.

Another example lay in his sporting achievement: undaunted by his isolated upbringing on a remote farm, and realising that his elder sisters were not interested in Rugby Football, he acquired a Rugby ball and a coaching book from the library: by practising assiduously in fields, he made himself into an excellent place kicker. Likewise he developed into a ferocious tackler, with a tackle bag made from old sacks and hung from a tree. This tackle bag did double duty as a punch bag, while he taught himself to box.

By the age of eighteen, he had played as a Wing Forward for the Leicester first team. He then went on to play for a great range of teams – Blackheath Moseley, Saracens, Windsor and principally for the Harlequins, in addition to two-timing two County sides, Sussex and Berkshire 'it seemed much easier to play for them both than to explain the mix-up' he unconvincingly claimed with that mischievous twinkle in his eye.

Despite irrefutable evidence to the contrary, Philip did not think of himself as an excellent Rugger player, or boxer (he boxed for the Army) or athlete (he represented his County and the Milocarians), or squash player (for the Jesters' Club). He never mentioned his own contributions – he thought only of the team's achievements and the spirit in which the game was played.

After spending an idyllic year of University sporting and social life as an undergraduate of Christ Church in 1933, he received a nasty jolt, when the authorities sent him down for omitting to pass his exams. 'Always learn from experience' he said, and did, taking care never to make the same mistake again. Rapidly finding himself a job as a prep school master, he won a scholarship to Cambridge in 1936 and graduated from St Catharine's College in 1939.

The impending war soon broke and Philip enlisted in the Royal Corps of Signals. [It gave him great pride forty years later to write the regimental history *The Vital Link,* at the request of General David Horsfield and with his collaborator Colonel Robin Painter.]

He saw action in the Far East, defending Malaya and Singapore island, where he and 60,000 other Allied troops were compelled to surrender to the Japanese and became a Prisoner of War for three and a half years.

That he felt betrayed and frustrated by the Allied command and the treachery and complicity of the politicians can be seen in his 1988 book, *World War II: The Untold Story:* 'for the British Government, and for Churchill in particular, it was an incredible disaster; to those who had been trying to make a fight of it the whole campaign had been a major exercise in frustration. The final insult was that the world blithely accepted the Japanese figures for the numbers who had surrendered and the absurdly inflated figure of 130,000 passed into history – in fact the true figure was 60,000'.

You would not find Philip making this statement anywhere else, as he would not talk about the past. He did however write about it revealingly – as in *The Fields of War* (1977) – 'When fighting soldiers eventually read or hear what was supposed to have taken place on campaigns in which they were engaged they tend to smile cynically. Sometimes they consider offering a few corrections, but rarely bother; the task, they often feel, is too large, and scarcely worth the trouble.'

As a PoW, Philip drew his strength from his background and his upbringing. He kept himself as fit and healthy as he could, remained resolutely positive in outlook and inspired his comrades with his unflagging belief that they would pull through.

To raise morale he organised theatrical productions and skits. Without props, scenery, paper, with people at the end of their powers of endurance, he still managed to put on entertainments to cheer the troops, to the complete incomprehension of the Japanese guards.

In one talk, a man who had been employed as a butler in a grand household described his day, eating meals both before and after waiting on the family 'he had two breakfasts, elevenses, two luncheons, high tea twice, and of course two dinners before absentmindly munching the dog biscuits he had pocketed as he took Her Ladyship's Chihuahua out for its nightly walk'. This to a rapt audience of PoWs whose daily ration was half a cupful of rice.

At the end of the war, Philip weighed four and a half stone, but he had survived. He set about building a new life, first at The Treasury, then at the British Council in Spain.

In 1948, with a young wife Patricia, and a newly-minted daughter, Diana (my brother and I were still ideas) he became a Junior Lecturer at the newly established RMA Sandhurst. This occupation of lecturing to young and stimulating young cadets – as well as the ideas that they gave back to him – fitted his abilities perfectly. He firmly believed and communicated that 'you could learn anything, if you put your mind to it' and that 'everybody was best at something, it was just a question of finding out what it was'. His forward leaning walk and his leadership by example appealed to cadets. He worked here for 31 years until his retirement, relishing his colleagues, the intake of cadets, the opportunities for sport and for coaching, and the grounds.

And to a man who was committed to the principle of working and playing 'full tilt', he relished the chance that the Sandhurst academic terms gave him to use 'what would otherwise have been my leisure' for his other interests.

Thirty one years amounts to more than a third of his life. During this time, he rose to be senior lecturer, teaching many intakes of cadets about politics and current affairs.

He immersed himself in the Academy's sport: he ran the Rugby XV and taught goalkicking to the then current England full back, John Willcox. He ran the athletics too, watching with immense satisfaction when his protégé, the Ghanaian Kotei, qualified for the Olympic high jump at the Sandhurst Athletic Ground, still wearing his track suit top.

He loved the relaxed concentration that fly fishing on the Sandhurst lake demanded. Deeming it a suitable activity for cadets, he would declare regretfully to each new intake that – as he was both the Secretary of the Fishing Club and the person responsible for deciding who passed their exams – the lists inevitably got muddled up. This rapidly boosted membership.

It would be a matter of great delight to him to know that Sandhurst has given permission for his ashes to be scattered over the pool on the Wish Stream named after him (the 'Plum' pool), where he fished only a month ago. 'How marvellous' he said then, 'to be able to still tie on a fly and to cast a good distance – and I'm 86!'

He relished teaching generations of cadets about both current affairs and how to communicate – till his time a neglected subject. He enjoyed drawing out from each individual what made him tick, habitually asking each new student to talk for a brief time in front of the class on subjects of their choosing. Cadets responded such diverse subjects as how to soft boil an egg and how to remove the top from a bottle of champagne in one blow from a sword.

Whatever the subject, the aim was to give self-confidence to these young officers. Eventually, it led to his founding a new and now thriving department of Communications. Begun as a small section within the Department of Political and Social Studies in 1973, it now has transformed into one of the three Academic Departments within Sandhurst's training.

Philip's great break came in 1967, at a time when he very much needed one: overburdened with school fees and with a very ill wife (Pat was to die in 1971), he took with both hands an introduction to a book publisher provided by his friend and Sandhurst colleague, Brigadier Peter Young. He never forgot this kindness and determined to repay Peter's faith in him. Seizing his opportunity of a contract and an advance, he saw a way to pay for his children's education and proceeded to write two books a year 'from a standing start' for the next twenty-five years.

That was a fantastic achievement – 150,000 published words, aside from the pages he crossed out or rejected, plus all the historical research – 3,000 words a week, every week for quarter of a century. 'You have to keep pushing the pen across the paper' he would say.

Every one of those words was lovingly and meticulously typed, and retyped if he wished, by Freda. It was just as well, as only Freda could read Philip's handwriting, which resembled most of the time the tracks of inebriated and exhausted sand eels, improving for a brief period every few months as he laboriously worked from a *Teach Yourself Handwriting* manual.

Many of the fifty or so books he has written have – to his great delight – come back into print in new formats as military classics. He felt that they were good books, his earnings from Public Lending Right reflecting library borrowings showed how often they were taken out, and now even publishers have seen the light. 'Never underestimate the stupidity of publishers, Dickie.'

Though each book was a massive labour – he would just say 'toil and swink', each one allowed Philip to describe events through the eyes of the soldier at the time, rather than looking 'with the benefit of hindsight'. In the *Crimean War* (1972), he says: 'Equally full of martial spirit, strategic foresight and tactical ability are critics who have never heard a shot fired in war, never endured hunger, thirst, heat or cold, and never commanded anyone, in war or peace, in their entire lives'.

This constant theme informed his biographies of unfashionable subjects, whose leadership styles he admired: for example, General Brian Horrocks 'The General who led from the front' and Field Marshal Claude Auchinleck 'The Lonely Soldier'…. lonely he may have been, but he had the vision which allowed the SAS to get started.

This empathy with his subjects and his ability to pick out the essential character of the people he wrote about led to a life and career that can be looked back on not only with great affection but an historian's eye for truth – no matter where the awkward facts might lead.

Philip Warner – a concise bibliography

Philip wrote many books across the military range. The following titles are being re-published as both print books and e-books. Please contact us with any queries:

Alamein
Auchinleck – The Lonely Soldier
Battle of France 1940
Battle of Loos
Best of British Pluck
British Battlefields – A complete Compendium
British Battlefields – Vol 1 – The South
British Battlefields – Vol 2 – The North
British Battlefields – Vol 3 – The Midlands
British Battlefields – Vol 4 – Scotland & The Border
British Battlefields – Vol 5 – Wales
Battlefields of The English Civil War
Battlefields of The Wars Of The Roses
Crimean War
Dervish: The Rise and Fall of An African Empire
Distant Battle
D Day Landings
Famous Welsh Battles
Field Marshal Earl Haig – The Enigma
Fields of War – Letters Home from The Crimea
Firepower
Growing Up in the First World War
Guide to Castles in Britain
Guide to Castles in Britain (Illustrated)
Harlequins
Horrocks – The General Who Led From the Front
Invasion Road
Kitchener – The Man Behind the Legend
Medieval Castle
Passchendaele
Phantom
Secret Forces of World War II
Sieges of the Middle Ages
The Soldier: His Life in Peace and War
Special Air Service, The SAS
Special Boat Squadron, The SBS
Stories of Famous Regiments, The
World War I: A Chronological Narrative
World War II: The Untold Story
Zeebrugge Raid

www.ingramcontent.com/pod-product-compliance
Lightning Source LLC
Chambersburg PA
CBHW052157090426
42741CB00010B/2307